ABANDONED IN HENDERSON

Steven T. Koecher Disappears at High
Noon Sunday, December 13, 2009

Arlo Hunter

Copyright © 2023 Arlo Hunter.
All Rights Reserved.

No Part of this book may be produced, stored in a retrieval system, or transmitted by any means without the written permission of the author.

ISBN: 978-1-917116-18-3

Dedication

First and foremost, I wish to dedicate this work to Steven T. Koecher. Wherever you are Steven, may God assist those who are looking to find you. May you be found soon and rest in a calm, tranquil and peaceful place. And to the Koecher family, I wish to express my sincere, heartfelt sorrow, for your loss.

Acknowledgment

I would be remiss if I did not acknowledge the long hours, hard work and research put together by one fine investigator. He knows who he is. To him, I take my proverbial hat off and say thank you. And to one other stellar investigator, he also knows who he is. Thank you for allowing me into your investigative world. I have learned much from your mentoring, teaching, and friendship. And to my patient wife for encouraging and supporting me in this endeavor. Thank you!

About the Author

The author often describes himself as "an average person" His roots are firmly planted in the Beehive state, having brought up three fine children, two sons, and a daughter, all adults now and living out their own lives. He retired after over 30 years as a telephone company employee. His passion as of late is working in his yard and caring for his two majestic greyhounds. Quite by accident, he became enthralled with the Koecher case after becoming a private investigator in 2017. It is his hope police will take another hard look at this case.

Table of Contents

Dedication i
Acknowledgment ii
About the Author iii
Disclaimer: vi
Preface viii
Chapter 1: How I Found Myself Here 1
Chapter 2: Steven's Background and Movements Prior To Disappearing 9
Chapter 3: An Anomalous Road Trip 12
Chapter 4: Overton, NV. And Henderson, NV. 16
Chapter 5: The Abandoned Cavalier 21
Chapter 6: Henderson and St. George Police Investigate 23
Chapter 7: Interview with One Retired Detective 35
Chapter 8: Koecher Sightings 37
Chapter 9: Exclusive Investigations 40
Chapter 10: The Landlord, Guns, Drugs, And A Stolen Porsche 44
Chapter 11: Background of Roommate J.Z. 49
Chapter 12: M.D.'s Background 53
Chapter 13: The Sleuth R.M. 55
Chapter 14: Armchair Detectives 59

Chapter 15: A Tarot Card Reading 77

Chapter 16: The Reading, February 17, 2011 79

Chapter 17: A Time Out 94

Chapter 18: 7 Podcast Episodes 96

Chapter 19: Interview with Sam DeMann, Mitch DeMann's Father 99

Chapter 20: Interview with MD 111

Chapter 21: Interview with A Landlord 146

Chapter 22: Las Vegas Bound 192

Disclaimer:

This narrative is a fact-based account of the circumstances surrounding the disappearance of Steven T. Koecher. It is based on actual evidence gathered to date.

The real names of persons considered "of interest," have been changed to pseudonyms. However, the initials used are factually correct.

The name of the investigative agency and its investigators are also pseudonyms. The police investigators mentioned in official reports, George Knapp, David Charns and David Paulides, are real.

Preface

"It won't happen to me."

Will someone please explain to me how a thirty-year-old person can be seen on a home's security video, driving his Chevrolet Cavalier into an over 55, large, so-called retirement community neighborhood, located in Henderson, Nevada, in the middle of a clear day? Then recorded on the same security video, walking with intention on the street with nearly no trees, with nice homes bordering on both sides, and he goes missing? Here one minute and gone the next. His empty vehicle, discovered days later. How is that even possible? How mind boggling.

Not only is it indeed possible, it actually happened to Steven T. Koecher on December 13, 2009, at noon, just as I described to you here. A piece of new evidence has come to light recently, including a previously unknown neighbor, who, at that time, lived very near to where Steven disappeared. This neighbor tells investigators he spoke to Steven on the day just before he disappeared. Additionally, interviews with already known persons, in this case, reveal subtle clues about what may have happened to Steven that day.

Could you be thinking right about now, oh,,, that won't ever happen to me!? Do you truly believe that? You may think something like this won't happen to you, but the realities of life are far from being safe, fair, and just. Terrible things happen to good people all the time. The truth is, it can happen to anyone, at any given moment, at any point in their lives. Just like the terrible occurrence that befell the Koecher family in December, 2009.

For all I, or anyone knows, "it won't happen to me" is your mantra. How unfortunate, this had to happen to "that poor boy," you might be thinking. I would consider that to be a good thing, I suppose. At a minimum, that would make you an empathic individual to some degree, right? You at least have a sense that a tragedy has occurred.

And yet, empathic is all you can be, right? We're powerless to do anything. I know there's not a-lot we can do. Or is there? Ever heard of a 'thought experiment'? Try this one with me, please. Consider for just a minute that you have not heard from, talked to, or even seen a person you love and care about for what seems to be an unusual amount of time. A beloved family member or best friend forever, perhaps. Do you become curious as to why? Do you reach the conclusion this is really out of character for them?

Their previously known, almost semi-predictable behavior appears obviously out of whack. What's going through your mind about this time? I could reach out; I could call or text, you think. When you call and or text, you find the call only goes to voicemail, and the texts are not returned. Ok, no biggie; they're probably busy, on vacation, or just away from their phone, right? I hope they are okay; you think to yourself. Then randomly, from out of nowhere, you notice an unfamiliar number calling on your cell phone. "I don't know who that is, you think, or even say out-loud."

Should you answer it or let the unknown Caller go to

voicemail? It could be your friend or loved one, couldn't it? Okay, so you've chosen to answer; of course, you have. The Caller then begins identifying themselves as a police officer in a particular city. They are calling to inform you a car has been found unattended, which happens to belong to that someone you're trying to reach. You're then told it's located somewhere which makes no sense to you.

What are you going to do next?

Understandably, you are surprised, maybe shocked too, no doubt. The worrisome circumstances you feel up to now then quickly change to, oh my God! Their car has been found where? That makes no sense for them to do that. What are they doing there? How do you begin to feel? Are you trying not to panic?

"They'll be back; probably nothing to worry about", "the car probably broke down, or maybe someone stole it," you might tell yourself. You're attempting to rationalize, trying to figure out, and asking yourself, "what the hell is going on here right now!"

At the same time, you're trying to cope as best you can with this shocking and surreal situation. I mean, really! Someone you love or care very much about is missing? Do you begin incessantly calling their cell phone, having it only go to voicemail again? You leave multiple messages, of course, "they may call back," you're hoping.

The feeling of anxiety becomes overwhelming. Wow!! Wow... breathe...just breathe! You might decide then to reach out to everyone you know for help. Thankfully, help eventually comes. Your family, friends, brothers and sisters, colleagues, cousins, aunts, and uncles all are coming together to provide support and assistance for you and your family.

After some time, and in an anxiety-laden, foggy state of mind, you think to yourself, "something has to be done," so you and your family members, along with your friends, and any other caring person who wishes to help, begin to look everywhere for him or her. Places that make sense, even places that don't make sense, are searched by car and on foot, and known acquaintances are called by phone, and messaged on social media.

There is an historical and relevant pattern of conduct that has emerged in many other cases which begin exactly this way. You would most certainly make up numerous fliers with the help of friends and sympathetic volunteers and place them everywhere. Eventually, and necessarily, of course, you go to a law enforcement agency and report your loved one as a missing person. Depending on the location of the disappearance, a search and rescue team might even be deployed bringing canines, helicopters, and dozens of search volunteers commonly known as "ground pounders," to help in the search.

The local media is contacted, and this story becomes part of a news cycle; maybe the story is even broadcast nationwide. You would hope it is. The story includes a picture of your loved one's face, describing their hair color, eye color, height, weight, any distinguishing marks, tattoos, or scars, where they were last seen, and what they may have been driving. Social media posts are made including all the above. A wide net is cast just in case someone has seen him or her and knows where they are. And yet, sadly, your loved one continues to still be missing. This horrific, baffling scene has been, and continues to this day, to be played out over and over, many, many times every year. It's actually an unbelievable and incomprehensible common occurrence where people go missing every year. The circumstances I have just described happened to the Koecher family in December 2009. If this scenario has played out in real life for you, and you are reading this, I want to say, "I'm sorry; I'm genuinely so sorry."

I try to imagine in my own mind someone disappearing who's close to me, what I would do, and how I would handle such a scenario. I would have no choice but to do the same, I suppose. What else could I do? But of course, hearing about or reading about someone else's plight isn't the same as actually having gone through it yourself, now is it? I am genuinely sad for the Koecher's, and that's one reason why I write about this heartbreaking story.

Forgive me for the following cliche', but if someone from the future, lets say, had visited me ten years ago, telling me, "you're going to get involved in the disappearance of Steven Koecher," I would say what? Are you crazy? First, probably because they're telling me they're from the future, right? They must be crazy. Second, maybe they're not crazy, and they really are from the future. They have come to warn and prepare me in some way.

As it came to pass, I could not help but finding myself captured by some sort of intrigue tractor beam pulling me into the Steven Koecher disappearance case, in 2017. It's been a time-consuming, laborious, and a huge learning experience for certain.

Indeed, a challenge to my ability to get most, if not all, of this story, on paper and in book form. How does Steven Koecher, a college educated, church going, bright young man, with his whole life ahead of him, just walk out of sight and into thin air? How does it even occur that entities, who should protect us, can be apathetic to it? Does that strike you as odd too? This is where we find ourselves, I guess in today's world.

My goal here and my subsequent reward, I pray, is documenting this sad ordeal the best I can, generating more leads, and getting more people talking, including the Henderson police. And above all, finding the truth of what really happened to Steven. It may be cliché to say, but I'm going to say it anyway, "someone knows something."

The agonizing truth of this circumstance is, Steven is likely viewed as just one person, one person amongst the other millions of people, and by simply not knowing Steven, he is a nobody in the eyes of most. Just another kid who went missing. That's too bad. But he was still a person, a young man with potential, a young man with a family, a young man who had friends, and a young man who had a future. And Poof! He's gone. Allow me to shine some light on some of the known facts in this case and some facts which may not be known.

Let's conduct a close examination together using some of the evidence gathered so far, and see if we reach the same conclusion, shall we? But first, I politely ask that you humor me for a while as I provide some background of my own.

Chapter 1:
How I Found Myself Here

In the early spring of 2017, I began getting some mean texts on my own phone from out of nowhere. I won't go into the substance of the text other than to say they were inappropriate. I dismissed them as junk at first.

A "Robo call" or a wrong number, maybe, I thought. Someone just messing with me would have been my last choice, but it turned out to be the correct choice. I had no idea who I was dealing with or what their motive was either. I responded to one or two of these texts, asking them to please mind their own business. Okay, I may not have said please, but I did mention minding their own business. I wasn't sure if I would get a response back, not knowing the source of the texts and all, but they did respond back to me with some snide remarks, which told me they were an ass for one, and two, this wasn't just a one-way communication, like a bot or something. The texts went on for a couple of days, and then to my surprise and chagrin, texts began to appear on a family member's phone. I knew right then it was time to do something about it. A phone number is all I had, but that was somewhere to start. Ironically, in a twist of fate, it seems, these mean texts would be the beginning of the whole Koecher case snowball effect for me.

I'll explain how, as I get us back to that number I had. Like many of you might have done, I conducted my own cursory investigation of sorts by Googling the phone number. If you've ever done this before, then, of course, you know this didn't turn up much of anything useful. I assumed it was a burner phone, something akin to a Walmart throwaway phone. Not to besmirch Walmart, of course; I shop there often.

Once upon a time, I had once used a private investigator in the past for a personal matter, and the idea occurred to me, why not use one here? I did what most of us would do; I Googled private investigators. Isn't Google wonderful? It's been asked, how can God answer all of the prayers God gets? The same question can be asked of Google, I suppose, when it is able to answer all of the inquiries that come into it every second. Moving on, my Google search resulted in several businesses advertising as "Private Investigations."

The first two I called went to voicemail. (Voicemail; an inefficient method of conducting a business such as a private investigator, in my humble opinion, but I digress.) I continued making calls to the listed investigators shown on my laptop screen. To my amazement, one answered on the first or second ring. Wow! How often does that happen in Today's business world? I mean, a human being answering the phone? Get outta here!

The fact that an actual person answered my call impressed me greatly, especially on the first or second ring. I introduced myself, told my story, and said all I had was a phone number.

I was pleasantly surprised when this person agreed to look into the matter right then. In a brief state of disbelief, I gave him the number I had and sent his requested $25 via PayPal.

He said he'd get back to me. And he did. Sometime later that day, I received a call back from this P.I. telling me what I already knew. This was most likely a "ghosted" number or a burner phone. A ghosted number is achieved by using software that masks one's own phone number and shows the receiver another number is calling.

Since I had already established there was two-way communication between this phantom and me, I asked this P.I. if he would formulate a text and, in it, educate this phantom of the laws broken, the consequences of breaking such laws, and that he possess the ability to track down and identify who they are. Turns out this P.I., I would later learn, was a retired police detective with thirty years of law enforcement experience.

Jackpot!

He agreed to my texting proposition. After proofreading his proposed text, I had him send it off to the phantom. The results were such that I never received another mean text, nor did my family member from the phantom afterward. I called the P.I. to thank him for his help. During our conversation, we talked about his business at some length. Fascinated by it all, I remarked, "I've always been interested in P.I. stuff, and if you needed anyone to help out, I would be interested," I said.

He explained to me he could use someone occasionally to serve legal papers or conduct surveillance, but his business was in a slow time right now. He'd get back to me, he said. Still interested, I followed up with phone calls or texts a few times over the weeks. A couple of weeks later, he and I spoke on the phone, and we agreed to meet for an interview in a local coffee shop.

I must have made an impression in the meeting because shortly thereafter, I became an apprentice private investigator. (An apprentice P.I., as described by Utah law, must be supervised by an Agent PI. Basically, a supervised private investigator or protégé.)

That was in March 2017, and at first, I found this new venture invigorating, interesting, and exciting. What's not exciting about following someone who doesn't know they are being followed? This is known as mobile surveillance. This can either be in a car or on foot. I've done both. Stationary surveillance is sitting in one's car in a neighborhood, watching a house or in a business parking lot, waiting for the subject to appear whereupon, as they walk out and I would "get the shot."

There were times when I would also serve legal documents to folks who tried very hard to avoid being served court papers. One story I tell is about serving someone who was avoiding service. I dressed up like a utility worker, wearing a hard hat, safety vest, and a tool belt with tools and knocked on their door. When they answered the door, I said, "I'm working in the neighborhood, are you the Jones'?" When they said yes, I said, "I have some paperwork for you," and handed the papers to them. Then I briskly walked away. I once used a pizza delivery ruse with the legal docs in the pizza box.

As time went by, and case after case was investigated, I found that being a private investigator is not like the one portrayed on T.V. No, I'd say my experience as a P.I. is many hours of sitting in a hot or cold car, parked in a neighborhood for hours, and having the neighbors do what I call "eyeballing" me. You may do it yourself sometimes when you notice a strange, out-of-place car parked near or in front of your home. You eyeball them for a minute, making an assessment of who they are and why they are there. I do it. I always have. While sitting in my car on surveillance, I've actually had neighbors even approach my car and ask, "What are you doing parked in front of my house?" I've always thought that as a weird, rather risky behavior in today's world.

In answering back, I would attempt to dismiss them with some sort of back story, "I'm investigating a missing person who has been reported to be in this location," I might say. In tailing, or following persons in their car, the P.I. is subjected to heavy traffic, stop lights, and people driving the speed limit for hell's sake, causing the person I'm following to make a green light but leaving me behind waiting for the now red light to change to green. As I wait, I watch them drive away and out of sight, losing them.

Losing a subject in traffic can be very frustrating. The feeling can be one of failure, but it is just part of the job. Took me several losses to get used to the feeling of failing. In a perfect world, or the world of law enforcement for example, there might be two to three other cars helping follow a subject, along with a helicopter flying overhead with everyone involved communicating on radios. Not a perfect world for the lone P.I., though. He or she is almost always alone, sometimes for hours on end, yet maintaining communication via cell phone with the agent who hired the P.I.

On the plus side, it is very rewarding when circumstances

align just right, such as good weather, light traffic, green lights, good location, and being in the right place at the right time. The reward is getting exactly what is requested. An example of getting exactly what is requested is getting some good video of someone claiming injury for the insurance money and capturing them at the gym exercising, doing yard work at their home, or jogging in the wee hours of the morning.

There are, of course, cheaters. Cheating is big business in the P.I. world. Nothing says cheating more than recording a make-out session between two persons, and neither is the recognized legal spouse of the other. I'll share one story of just that kind of situation. Using GPS tracking technology, I found a couple behind a small shopping mall one night at about 10 PM, their two cars parked side by side. It was obvious what was going on. I put on a safety vest and a hat, along with a fake, I.D. attached to the vest. I had my camera in one hand and a flashlight in the other as I walked up to the car they were both in. Once I arrived at the car, and in a loud voice, I said, "this is security, you can't be here!" and shined the flashlight into the back seat and recorded the couple doing what couples do in the backseat of a car. The video I shot said it all.

Just some examples of the many different kinds of cases I've investigated. The stories I could tell. I've said many times, "I'd rather be lucky than good." When being lucky and being good come together at the same time, they blend into a rare recipe for success, and the taste is sweeter than dark chocolate when it all goes right. I've heard the word "luck" defined as; preparation coupled with opportunity. It is so true. Being prepared and being in the right place at the right time is akin to making par in golf, or bowling a perfect game. Then, of course, comes all the documentation that follows; the report writing and video processing, all need to be completed in a timely manner.

A time-consuming, technically frustrating, at times, yet necessary part of the job. Good report writing is pleasing to an agent's eye and necessary for an attorney to successfully argue the case later in court.

After around a year of working with this retired law enforcement officer, now a private investigator agent (An agent is described by Utah law as someone having 5000 hours of experience or its equivalent,) a potential new investigator had applied to work on the team in 2017. James Baker was a newly retired F.A.A. investigator.

He interviewed with the aforementioned P.I. agent. The agent, or boss, rightly thinking that this former F.A.A. agent's investigatory experience would be helpful. Hired him on and put him to work. He would come aboard as a registrant private investigator. (A registrant P.I. is described by Utah law as having 2500 hours of experience or the equivalent,)

A registrant is basically an unsupervised private investigator. James would now sit in his car, follow and lose his subjects, serve court documents and write his own reports like the rest of us. Coincidentally, as it turns out, this retired F.A.A. investigator somehow knew the Steven Koecher family. And hearing that James was now a P.I., a Koecher family member approached him asking to look into Steven's disappearance.

He righteously took on the case and approached the team for assistance. Up to this point, I had not even heard of Steven, or the Koecher case. I was, however, very intrigued at the thought of investigating a missing person.

It was after James started his investigation that I got my first introduction to the now well-known video footage of Steven Koecher, the missing person, walking by a home with security cameras on it in Henderson, Nevada. The security cameras were on the home, whose owner at that time was a retired air marshal. I watched this video footage as it apparently shows Steven Koecher arriving on Savannah Springs Ave, in his 2003 Chevrolet Cavalier, at 11:54:10. At 12:00:10, Steven is seen walking into view, walking east on Savannah Springs.

Then turning north onto Evening Lights, where he's then seen in a reflection on a parked car window from another camera angle on the same house. He crosses east on Evening Lights and continues north. My first question was, "Is that even Steven?" The other question, which did not resonate with me until sometime later, was, "what could Steven have been doing during those 6 minutes after arriving and then walking into view?" More on that later. The video recording was probably recorded in a 720P resolution. Not great, but good enough. The family tells James they are certain it is Steven in the video. This became the start of the bug biting me and not letting go. I was forever intrigued.

Chapter 2:
Steven's Background and Movements Prior To Disappearing

Victimology is the study of the victim and gathering as much information about them as possible. In this case, Steven Koecher is the victim. Who was Steven? What was his relationship with his family like? Where was he going? Who did he associate with? What caused him to be in Henderson? How and why did he go missing? All relevant questions in victimology. I will attempt to address those questions here based on our investigation.

Who is Steven T. Koecher?

Steven T. Koecher was born in Amarillo, Texas, on November 1, 1979. He is one of four children of Rolf and Deanne Koecher. He had just turned 30 about a month prior to his disappearance. As a small child and then an adolescent, Steven became a Boy Scout first, then became an Eagle Scout. He was most likely baptized into the LDS church record at age 8, 9, or 10 years old. He graduated from Amarillo High School in 1998. He was a devoted member of the LDS church. Steven attended Ricks College (now BYU-Idaho), after which he attended the University of Utah, where he received a degree in communications. He served a mission for the LDS Church in Brazil and spoke Portuguese.

Stop and think of the people Steven must have spoken with

and maybe even baptized there. After college, Steven interned in the office of the then Governor of Utah for 9 months. Sometime later, he went to work for the Davis County Clipper in Bountiful. The Clipper was edited by his father at the time. Some articles Steven worked on even received awards from the Utah Press Association.

In 2007, Steven began working for the Salt Lake Tribune's digital advertising division. Steven did not like the overnight shifts, and coupled with the climate and temperature inversions Salt Lake City is known for; he left the Tribune for a warmer climate in St. George, UT. Shortly after arriving in St. George, Steven found a home in which he rented one room. Another renter, who I'll call Justin Zimmer, or J.Z., was already renting one of the other bedrooms in the home when Steven arrived. The owner of the home at the time was a man who I'll call Big Ben. Big Ben, or B.B., kept a room there for his own use and used the home's garage for storage. He reportedly told J.Z. he would hardly ever be there. However, according to Steven's roommate Justin Zimmer this was not the case.

During the time of the "Great Recession," Steven found it difficult to find work in St. George. He found a means of earning some income by handing out window-washing fliers for a local window-washing firm. Some of these flyers would later be found in Steven's so-called abandoned car. This particular job, it seems, was insufficient to provide the essential income to meet Steven's obligations. I can only imagine how frustrating it must have been for Steven, a college-educated young man, who made such a bold and brave geographical move to St. George, searching for a new life, only for the economy to pull the proverbial rug out from under him, leaving Steven in the quandary he was in. By November 2009, Steven reportedly became three months delinquent in the rent.

This landlord, to which Steven owed back rent to, was a person who Las Vegas metro law enforcement knew well. Later it would be found, via background checks, that B.B. had a record of drugs, guns, and an ill-acquired stolen Porsche. In addition, it is reported B.B. may have been involved in a legitimate "closed-door pharmacy" along with two other associates. A closed-door pharmacy is a pharmacy that only dispenses medication to a select group of patients and does not provide its services to the broader patient population. It is not eligible to be registered as a wholesale distributor. Additionally, most closed-door pharmacies provide their customers with a delivery service for their orders. A delivery service? That sounds interesting, doesn't it?

Chapter 3:
An Anomalous Road Trip

On December 9, 2009, Steven attended a "Ward Temple Night" in St George, UT. Witnesses confirm Steven was there around 6:30 PM. It's still unclear when exactly, whether before, during, or after this event is when Steven's landlord contacts Steven's father using the contact information from Steven's rental agreement. B.B. informs Steven's father of Steven's back rent situation.

Steven's father and Steven then have a conversation over the phone to talk about this rent situation. Steven seems to have become irritated by the fact his father has been brought into his lacking rent quagmire, so much so that during the conversation with his father that night, Steven hangs up on him. What can we imagine Steven is feeling at this moment? Anger, frustration, embarrassment, scared, perhaps a feeling of desperation too? I don't know, but I do know how I feel when the income is in short supply compared to the expenses.

It is also unknown exactly when Steven begins an unannounced, widely reported, and somewhat of a strange trip toward Salt Lake City, then on to Wendover, UT., and finally landing in Ruby Valley, NV. Ruby Valley is approximately 100 miles south of Wendover, NV. The best guess anyone seems to have is that the strange trip started either late on the 9th or in the early hours of December 10.

This strange trip he takes is well documented using

recovered store receipts from his car, his banking records, and interviews with family. Interviews with the family indicate Steven once met a girl who I'll identify only as A.M., while they both participated in a cattle branding event in April 2008 at a ranch in Ruby Valley, NV.

There is the appearance Steven simply traveled to Ruby Valley to see his friend A.M. However, when Steven arrived at the ranch at approx.12:00 PM on the 10th, A.M. was not at home at the time. He still visited with her family for approximately two hours, having lunch with them at the home and conversing. During their visit and conversation, Steven tells A.M. 's family, he is on his way to visit family in Sacramento, California, which appears untrue and a clue.

He went on to say he wasn't certain he should travel there due to the forecasted bad weather. After his approximate 2-hour visit, Steven makes his way back to St. George, backtracking over the same route he traveled to get there. Now why would Steven travel approximately 7 hours and cover 540 miles driving from St. George, UT. to Wendover, NV., then on to Ruby Valley, NV., to visit a friend without first knowing if she would be there when he arrived? That really makes no sense to me. It doesn't appear he ever reached out first to see if A.M. would even be there. He had a phone. Could it be that he didn't have her number? Somehow he had enough cash to buy fuel though. Something here seems off, Does it to you?

As Steven travels back, cell phone records indicate he received a cell phone call from his sister, and during their conversation, Steven does not mention this odd trip he is on. (Evidence of a fuel/snack purchase from a Tesoro fuel station in Salt Lake for $7.30, found on a bank statement.) Getting closer to St. George, Steven also speaks with his mother by cell phone for the last time. The two discuss future plans for Steven to come home to Bountiful for Christmas. Mrs. Koecher reports Steven seemed upbeat about spending Christmas with his family along with possible job prospects.

It's important to note here Steven had made future plans with his mother during this conversation, to be at a family gathering which he looked forward to attending. Another clue. He not only does not tell his sister, but he also does not tell his mother about either of the trips he had just almost completed. Another clue. (A receipt for fuel purchase, $32.88, Flying J in Springville, UT., is found in the empty car.) Later that afternoon, he visits Taco Time (a receipt from Nephi, UT, is found with a time stamp of 7:24 PM.) I'd be hungry, too, after driving for hours.

Using witness statements, food receipts, interviews, and cell phone records, it's estimated Steven had traveled around 1100 miles on that trip; why? To see an acquaintance in hopes of a possible romance with a woman he met at a cattle branding event? Maybe, but doesn't it make sense to first reach out over the internet or over the phone to see if AM would even be there? All that driving takes a toll on a person. The necessary thing for Steven to do after this trip is to sleep. I believe he had to, and I believe he did after arriving back in St. George. Where he slept is anyone's guess, in his car, or in his room at the house. He was known to sleep in his car at times.

Initially, when I looked at this trip, I saw it as Steven's attempt to blow off steam brought about by his dad's call about the back rent. It hurt his pride. He needed to clear his head, cool off, or get away from it all for a while and possibly just visit a friend to talk to.

My thinking has changed on that prospect. It may be just my thinking, but I'd call first to see if A.M. was even going to be there. Wouldn't you, before setting off on such a long drive? A couple of details about this trip struck me; 1) Steven lies to the family in Ruby Valley about what he's doing there; he's not traveling to Sacramento; 2) He does not tell either his mother or his sister about what he's doing when they talk on the phone. That makes no sense to me. What does make sense to me, having lived in the LDS community, shall we say? Steven is a proud family member, devout Mormon, respected by all who knew him, generous, helpful, and trying to live an independent, honorable Mormon lifestyle. "I can handle this in my own way with God's help," he might believe.

To me, this trip has the appearance of someone asking Steven to run an errand of some kind. Additionally, I don't believe for a minute that Steven is going to knowingly participate in any type of illegal errand; no. But, suppose Steven gets some kind of assurance this errand was legal? "Don't worry, it's all legal," he may have been told. This explanation made sense to Steven, and he trusted the messenger. Then perhaps, Steven might see the requested errand in a different light, questionable yet not illegal, and perhaps making some money in the process.

Chapter 4:
Overton, NV. And Henderson, NV.

Around 3:00 PM the next day, December 11, Steven is handing out fliers for the window washing firm in a St. George neighborhood when he encounters two young girls who had been locked out of their home after school.

Being the honorable LDS person he was, Steven came to their rescue by trying to call the girl's mother, having the call only go to voicemail, where he then left a message. This call Steven makes to the girl's mother is confirmed by Steven's cell phone records. In the end, he did fortunately find a neighbor who agreed to take the girls in until someone could get them into their own home. Good job, Steven! That same day, he buys food at a Jack-In-The-Box on Telegraph St, in Washington, UT. and speaks with his ward's Bishop, who is also trying to help Steven find a job.

The next morning, Saturday, December 12, 2009, for still unknown reasons, Steven leaves St. George and travels toward Las Vegas, where his phone pings off a cell tower near Overton, NV. Overton, NV., is located 78 miles from St. George and 28 miles southwest of Mesquite, close to the north end of Lake Mead.

In the evening of the same day, presumably traveling back to St. George, he bought gas and snacks at a convenience store in Mesquite, NV. This is verified using point-of-purchase receipts and bank records. It is unknown why or where Steven traveled to that day. All we can say is somewhere near Overton, NV. Three hours after the purchase of gas and snacks in Mesquite, Steven purchased Christmas gifts at a St. George K-Mart for his brother and family, whose names he had drawn for Christmas presents. After all, he planned on going home for Christmas (receipt from K-mart for $9.42, a child's bib, and 4 Christmas ornaments @ $1 each.)

This is a 6 to 8-hour day trip in my mind. Steven traveled to, or through Overton, NV., back to Mesquite, then returned to St. George; why? I don't know, but I see this as a trip somewhere, out there, either to meet someone to get instructions and/or picking up something which is to be delivered the next day, December 13, 2009. Or perhaps, this is a trial run in order to familiarize himself with a location or an address.

Could this location be where his car was later found empty? No one can explain why he traveled to Overton or Henderson. The question is, why did Steven's phone ping in Overton, NV.? Where did he go that day?

On the night of December 12, a neighbor of Steven's reports to the landlord of seeing Steven return to his home around 10 PM. And a half hour later, he left. Let me repeat that. "A half-hour later, he left." He was not seen returning. Now wait a minute; it's Saturday night at 10:30 PM; Steven is Mormon. Wouldn't it make more sense that he would want and need to attend church the next day, Sunday? This behavior is incongruent with Steven's personality, in my opinion.

It's 10:30 PM on a Saturday night, and this devout LDS

counselor goes out? Why? What goes through your mind?

The next morning, Sunday, December 13, 2009, a person I will call Good William (The L.D.S. Church Elder's Quorum President) is coincidentally driving out of Las Vegas that very same morning. He calls Steven at around 7:50 AM. G.W. asks Steven if he could help in conducting a church service to take place in St. George at 11 AM that morning. G.W. indicates he may not make it back in time. Steven tells G.W. he is also in Las Vegas but would return if he needed him to. G.W. tells Steven not to worry about it; he will handle the service. Call ends.

Another ward member, who I will call Sacred Agent, also called Steven two hours later to ask if Steven could attend a basketball game in St. George. Steven tells S.A., no, he's in Las Vegas. This part is odd, but it happened. Neither person asked Steven why he was in Las Vegas. Big wow!! For me. Should they have asked Steven why he was in Vegas? "What ya doin' in Henderson, Steven?" No one's being accused of anything here. It's just strange to me no one asked why he was in Las Vegas. "Oh, cool, Steven! Whatcha doin there?"

Three hours later, at 11:54 AM, a home security camera, on a home owned by a retired air marshal on Savannah Springs Ave, in Henderson, NV., records Steven's 2003 Chevy Cavalier driving west into a cul-de-sac in the Overlook Village of Sun City Anthem, where it would later be found empty at the end of Savannah Springs Ave. In the same video, a white SUV is captured traveling west past the security cameras, where it apparently makes a U-turn and stops on Savannah springs a few houses east. This was followed up on, and found out to be a real estate agent who was just there working.

Steven's car is recorded driving west on Savannah Springs Ave, past the security cameras and out of sight. Six minutes later, a male person, believed to be Steven by his family, who appears to be wearing a jacket, white shirt, and slacks, is seen walking into view from the west, rounding a corner, and turning north onto Evening Lights St. In the video it appears he is carrying something under his left arm. Hmmm, what could that be? What's your guess? Another camera from the same security system pointed toward Evening Lights captures Steven walking north on Evening Lights, appearing to walk across the street and toward the east side of Evening Lights. As Steven makes his way crossing the street, he can be seen in a car window reflection walking north on the east side of Evening Lights and out of view. Steven Koecher walks out of view and out of existence. He is never to be seen again.

Five hours after Steven seemingly walked into oblivion, at around 5:00 PM (according to cell phone records,) Steven's phone pinged off of a tower north of his last known whereabouts, near the intersection of Arroyo Grande Boulevard and American Pacific Drive. Using Google Earth, I was able to locate a cell tower near that intersection. It was one of those cell towers which is disguised to look like a tree. Two hours after that, his cell pinged off of a tower near Henderon's Whitney Ranch subdivision north of the previous ping. Again I was able to locate a tower there. The next morning, the phone pinged off of a tower at the interchange of Interstate 515/U.S. 93 and Russell Road, two more miles north of the last ping. Once more, I located a tower near that junction. Using the same cell phone records, there is a record of Steven's landlord (BB) calling Steven's phone and sending a text, then an hour later, it was used to check Steven's voicemail by someone. Possibly a close family member.

Steven's phone continued receiving calls and getting texts and remained in this last tower's vicinity for the next two days (December 15); presumably, this is when the battery went dead. What's the deal with the phone here? Is it logical and reasonable to say that the phone was carried there from Steven's last known location (on Evening Lights) by someone? Or carried there by something, or someone else, say a garbage truck or an accomplice? Did the phone travel with Steven, dead or alive?

One might want to speculate and say Steven walked north after abandoning his car. Maybe, I don't believe that. He or his body has never surfaced, and neither has his phone, nor his identification. Is he buried near the location where the phone died? Is it possible the phone was just tossed out of a moving vehicle and left in the dirt alongside the highway, where the battery died? The phone gets covered in debris and lost until discovered by accident sometime later. I suppose that's possible too, isn't it? These are all really good questions. Is it a coincidence there just happens to be a U-Haul storage complex and an Extra Space Storage complex very near 515 & Russell Road that I found on Google Earth?

Chapter 5:
The Abandoned Cavalier

Webster's definition of Abandon is-
"To give up with the intent of never again asserting an interest in (a right or property.)"

Three days later on December 16, parking enforcement personnel with the Overlook Village management take note of a car parked at the end of Savannah Springs and attempt to find the owner. Looking into the car and seeing some of the window washing fliers, they call the number from one of the fliers and reach the owner of the window washing firm Steven was associated with. The owner then calls Mr. and Mrs. Koecher, but he only gets voicemail, whereupon he leaves a message. On the 17th, Mrs. Koecher retrieves the voicemail, and the two parents immediately travel to Henderson. It's hard to imagine what must have been going through their minds as they traveled to Henderson. The questions, the strange circumstances, and right before Christmas too. It must have been a harrowing drive for them.

Upon arriving at the location of the "out of place," empty, so-called abandoned Cavalier, Mr. Koecher begins canvassing homes by going door to door. This is where he discovers the surveillance cameras on the home of the retired air marshal and secures the now-infamous Steven Koecher video. When Henderson police arrived, they reported finding "no evidence of foul play" and released the vehicle to Mr. and Mrs. Koecher on December 18, 2009.

Wait a minute, "No evidence of foul play?" I beg to differ here. These circumstances are completely out of context for Steven. Steven's empty car has been located in an over 55, upscale retirement community in Henderson, NV., and Steven is missing. Nothing makes any sense to the Koechers about the empty car, where it is located, or why he may have traveled there. The foul committed here is that Steven's parents, and his family, have now been thrust into what must have been extreme confusion and anxiety created by this nonsensical situation. Where is Steven?

Mr. Koecher attempted to report Steven as a missing person to the Henderson police, who arrived to investigate, but he was told by them he must do that in St. George since that is where Steven resided. Henderson police do check local jails and the morgue for Steven to no avail. Mr. Koecher checks local hospitals with negative results. He also speaks with associates and friends of Steven. Nobody knew where Steven was. Mr. Koecher stated to Henderson police, "Steven had only been to Las Vegas for a few vacations, and he did not know if Steven had any friends who lived there."

The police report states, "At this point, the connection to Steven coming to Las Vegas or Henderson is unclear." (It sure as hell is; I call foul!) Also, in the Henderson police report, Mr. Koecher states, "Steven had been having financial problems and was having problems making the rent in St. George." He goes on to say Steven had been given $500.00 on December 12, 2009, to help with bills. When Steven's account is accessed by Mrs. Koecher, she finds "there had been no activity on the account since the deposit, nor was his Facebook page showing any activity."

Chapter 6:
Henderson and St. George Police Investigate

On Friday, December 18, at 9:10 AM, a St. George police officer created and entered this synopsis: On 12/18/2009, I met with Steven's father and brother at the St. George police department. They had additional information regarding Steven and his activities. They had been able to get some credit card use information. Steven's card had been used in Wendover on 12/10. On 12/11, his card was used in St. George. On 12/12, it was used in Nevada, in St. George (at the K-mart), and in Salt Lake City. The charges were mostly at gas stations and were not for outrageous amounts. This evidence corroborates with the trip to Ruby Valley, back home, through, or to Overton, NV., and back home to St. George.

On December 23, 2009, a Henderson police detective entered a narrative in a report this way, "At this point, there is no explanation for Steven's actions or a reason why he ended up in Henderson before abandoning his vehicle. Steven was entered as a missing person by HPD dispatch, and this investigation is continuing."

The misnomer of using the word "abandoned" bothers me greatly here. Steven did not abandon his vehicle. He had every intention of returning to it. Remember, he made plans to return home for Christmas. His vehicle was quite simply empty, or unoccupied, and Steven was missing. Does using abandon here suggest that every time we leave our own vehicle, we are abandoning it? No, of course not. Using the word abandoned implies he was not returning to his car. When in reality, the evidence found in his car points to him returning to it, doesn't it?

In the St. George police report, this narrative appears:

"Mrs. Koecher contacted me via telephone and provided me with the following information. "She explained that an officer in Henderson, NV., found her son's vehicle. They informed her that the vehicle appeared to be abandoned." "She explained she was extremely worried because she had attempted to contact him numerous times by cell phone. She stated she contacted his landlord and asked him to check his welfare." "The landlord informed Mrs. Koecher that he had been looking for Steven for some time, too, because he was behind on rent. She stated she contacted all of Stevens's friends in the area as well but was unable to find anyone who knew where Steven was at this time." "She explained the landlord (B.B.) contacted a neighbor who informed him they saw Steven leaving his residence on the night of December 12, 2009." "The neighbor told the landlord that Steven said he was traveling to Las Vegas...."

"Mrs. Koecher explained that it was very odd that she had been unable to contact Steven." "She stated she had her cell phone company track Steven's phone." "She said the company was able to track everyone's phone except for Steven's. The phone company explained to Mrs. Koecher that they think Steven's cell phone battery is not charged, and this is why they can't track it."

In the St. George's police report, there is mention of a roommate Steven shared the house with. The report states, "The family told me that they had heard that Justin was from Chicago and had some trouble there, but seemed like a nice enough guy. They could not expound". When the officer spoke with Justin, Justin stated, "He has not lived with Steven for about a month. J.Z. states to the officer, "Steven was pretty upset about his work situation."

He tells police that he moved out because Steven was not able to pay his part of the rent, and he (J.Z.) could not have a roommate who could not pay their portion. When the officer asks the roommate about Steven's friends or associates he knew of, he tells the officer, "Steven associated with various persons from his ward."

The officer asked the family if they knew of any medical, mental, or emotional issues Steven may have had. "They did not know of any." However, Steven's father does say Steven once quit a job where he had to work the graveyard shift because he thought everyone was out to get him. Now I had to read that statement over and over again. Ask yourself here, how many of us may have had similar experiences during our own employment? I have at times. Some people are just hard to get along with. It's the nature of working with other people, many of whom we really don't know.

In a December 22, 2009, in an entry in the St. George police report, Mrs. Koecher says that after learning of the "abandoned" car, her husband immediately left for Henderson to find it. She states, "Her husband had found Steven's 2003 white Chevy Cavalier with all the doors locked with ½ tank of gas parked in a cul-de-sac in a retirement community." It was later discovered a blanket, and a pillow were in the car. Steven was known to sleep in his car at times.

After reading this, I wondered if Steven may have slept in his car somewhere in Las Vegas the night before he disappeared. The officer continues in his report, "During my conversation with Mrs. Koecher, she said that she had last spoken with Steven on December 10." (This would be during the return trip from Ruby Valley, NV.) "She stated their conversation consisted of Steven telling her of his financial troubles and that he was 3 months behind in his rent." "She mentioned that the last bank activity had been at a gas station in Mesquite, NV." This would have been the return trip from the Overton, NV. trip.

The report also details Steven's bank account activity describing how monies were deposited by Mrs. or Mr. Koecher in the account but remained untouched since deposited. When questioned about Steven's demeanor during the time of his financial troubles, Mrs. Koecher describes her son as "frustrated with not being able to find work." She denies that Steven was depressed or had ever spoken of suicidal ideations. She also had no knowledge of any friends Steven had in the Las Vegas area.

Continuing in the report; the Detective describes his viewing of the security video along with his reviewing of two cell phone calls made on December 13. The one from Good William, or G.W., and the one from the fellow counselor, Sacred Agent, or S.A., who asks about Steven's ability to attend a basketball game. The officer notes, "Both of these phone calls had corresponding latitude and longitude coordinates." "The first phone call at 0852 had a latitude of 35.2577778 and a longitude of -115.075. The second phone call at 1053 hours had a latitude of 35.9672222 and a longitude of -115.181944." He states, "I researched the latitude and longitude of the phone calls online. I found that the first set of coordinates returned to a location that was south of Henderson, and the second set of coordinates returned to a location on I-15 that was again south of Henderson."

When I first read about these coordinates, recorded in an official police report, mind you, I was excited to learn the locations, right? When I entered the second set of coordinates of the call made at 1053 hours in Google Earth (35.2577778 latitudes and -115.075 longitude), I was shocked at where they took me. This location is south of Henderson alright and appeared on Google Earth, in Hart, California, near an old abandoned gold mine and the Castle Mountains National Monument, approx. 47 air miles south of the Savannah Springs and Evening Lights intersection where he was last seen and his car was found. Well, someone needs to search there! I thought. Try as we did; we were, and still are not, able to confirm with the police if these coordinates are indeed accurate, even though they are in an official police report.

In closing his report, the Detective notes, "I called and spoke with Steven's Elder Quorum President (G.W.) to inquire about the conversation he had with Steven the morning of 12/12/2009." The Quorum President stated that he had called Steven to ask if he could attend a meeting for him since he was in Las Vegas. Steven told him that he was currently in Las

Vegas himself, but he could go back to St. George if needed." When questioned about Steven's demeanor during the call, G.W. tells the Detective, "He didn't notice anything unusual or suspicious while talking with Steven." The Detective also calls the counselor who called Steven about the basketball game. S.A. reported the same sense of Steven during their call that G.W. had sensed during his; nothing unusual.

On or about December 23, the Las Vegas Sun ran a story asking for the public's assistance. On the 24th, both Fox 5 Vegas and The Salt Lake Tribune ran a story asking for the public's help. Neither of these stories provided any good leads. A Facebook page was constructed by family and friends, also asking for help in locating Steven. The Anthem community had a local television channel, 99, which aired Steven's photo and information regarding his disappearance. We know now this didn't provide any good leads either.

On December 29, 2009, at approx. 2:00 PM, A Las Vegas Metro police Sgt. arranged for a metro helicopter to assist in searching the surrounding desert areas near the Anthem neighborhoods for Steven. They found nothing of any value in the case.

December 30, 2009, a Henderson detective makes contact with some of the residents in the area of Steven's last known location. It's remarkable to me that over two weeks later, this is the first and only indication I see of police canvassing homes in the neighborhood. Steven's father immediately started knocking on doors as soon as he arrived at the car.

One neighbor who was interviewed by police stated, "He'd

been contacted by the missing person's father and had no information in reference to Steven Koecher."

Now, another neighbor who lived on Evening Lights and who was interviewed by police provided some eye-catching details of happenings on that Sunday. She states, "She had been contacted by the missing person's father and said the neighborhood is generally quiet." She further stated, "She felt the neighbors across the street from her were acting unusually two weeks ago on a Sunday."

Which would have been the 13th. Furthermore, this neighbor states, "a large moving truck arrived, and that the residents moved a lot of boxes in approximately three hours; she has not seen the occupants of the residence since, and the white van that normally parks there has not been back." (she describes a "large moving truck," and "a white van, both there") Turns out this home she refers to is across the street from hers and very close to where Steven was last seen on the video, and on the same side of the street, he walked over to. Coincidence?

On December 31, 2009, police, along with two volunteers and a trained K-9, met with a city maintenance person who assisted in accessing flood channels, including underground tunnels in the Anthem neighborhoods which produced negative results.

January 6, 2010, Henderson police arrived at the home described by the neighbor across the street, as the suspicious house, to interview the residents of that home. The one where the neighbors were reported acting unusually and were moving a lot of boxes. Where a "large moving truck," and "a white van" were also observed.

After receiving no answer at the door, police leave one of Steven's missing person fliers. Returning later in the evening of the same day, police observed the flier had been removed and still met with negative contact at the front door.

A white Dodge van was observed parked in the driveway of the residence, bearing a Nevada plate which was returned to persons registered to that residence; I'll call them the DeMann's, Sam DeMann, of the DeMann family, He owned the van. Remember the white Dodge van. The question of a moving van vs a cargo van comes up later in an interview with Mitch. Would you have expected someone to come to the door if the Dodge was in the driveway?

Two days later, on January 8, 2010, at approx. 2:00 PM, Henderson detectives responded back, and noticed the Dodge van again parked in the driveway. Once more, they met with negative contact at the front door. Detectives leave a business card on the door requesting contact as soon as someone is home. The Detective notes in his report later, "I have still not received any telephone calls from the resident." (The DeManns are unaccounted-for, for 2 days?)

January 13, 2010, at around 1:30 PM, detectives located Sam DeMann, owner of the suspicious home at another residence, and interviewed him. (One month later.) They found Mr. DeMann at the new residence he presumably moved into. Sam DeMann states he saw the flier attached to the mailbox at his old house but did not recognize Steven. He also states he had already talked with uniformed officers along with a private investigator.

Curious, I have not seen, or recall reading anywhere, an entry by police about S.D. previously being interviewed. We do however, have an interview with the retired Detective where he states Sam was cooperative, letting them inspect the suspicious property. Sam goes on to explain his son, who I'll call Mitch DeMann, lives in the casita at the old address, and *he* did not recognize Steven either. Detectives ask to have his son Mitch contact them, whereupon Dad says he will tell him. They provide a number to call. According to the police, the son never called back.

Again, on January 15, 2010, Henderson detectives arrived once more at the suspicious home and received no contact at the front door, again. Another card was left requesting that Mitch DeMann contact them upon receiving the card. Again, the Detective states later, "As of this point, he has yet to contact me."

About the time this is all taking place, detectives secure Steven's laptop computer and, after obtaining a search warrant, forensically search it. The police report states, "Upon reviewing the laptop and searching internet history, there was nothing of evidentiary value located on the computer."

One month and 5 days later from the last "no contact," on February 18, 2010, at approximately 3:00 PM, Henderson detectives responded again to the suspicious home and finally located Mitch DeMann at the address and spoke with him. Pictures of Steven are shown to him. He viewed the pictures and stated to detectives, "I can't say that I have seen him." That is a curious statement, don't you think? "I can't say?" Why can't you say M.D.? He might as well have said, "I won't say, or I'm not going to say," instead of what someone with nothing to hide would say; "No, I haven't seen him." or "I'm sorry, I have not seen this person."

Detectives, being the trained observers they are, note in their report, "Mitch appeared to be nervous when contacted and while being questioned about Steven's disappearance." "He would relax at times while talking about his work project, but then became evasive when asked about where he was currently residing." "Mitch states he uses the casita as his address and will be moving back into it soon." (I ask myself here, did the police find Mitch in the big home, or the casita?) There is a casita located on the suspicious activity address in front of the main home..

The Detective continues in his report; "Mitch stated that he doesn't tell anyone where he lives. He doesn't have any friends in town and does not trust anyone due to the drug lifestyle that people tend to have." The Detective's observations they reported are a clue.

During this interview, detectives tell Mitch that Steven wasn't in any trouble and that he was only listed as missing, and we were trying to locate him. Detectives ran a scenario by Mitch, asking if Steven may have contacted him about finding work. Mitch responds with, "That didn't happen." Mitch states, "He did not recall seeing Steven's vehicle parked in the cul-de-sac for three days in December." Detectives ask Mitch what kind of work he did, and his reply is, "He did research and was currently developing a safety feature for the bus stops to keep people from getting hit by other vehicles while waiting."

From my perspective, this interview with M.D. is very telling, strange, and may very well be, one of the most momentous opportunities swung at and missed by police. In my humble opinion, M.D. should have been interviewed by police again, purely based on that interview alone. At least to establish his whereabouts on December 13, 2009, at about noon. Quite frankly, the question I would ask is this: "Mr. DeMann, can you account for your whereabouts on December 13, 2009, at noon?" Boom! That's the question. It never got asked, to my knowledge.

The same day, February 18, 2010, police made another entry into the report involving persons who many of you may be familiar with. The report states, "I was contacted by Steve Powell. Steve is the father of Josh Powell, whose wife {Susan Powell} was reported as a missing person on December 7. Steve stated he had information he wanted to email me showing similarities between his daughter-in-law's disappearance and Steven's. I did not receive the email and was contacted again on the 23rd by Steve.

Steve told me he was meeting with the FBI soon and would send the information after he spoke with them. On the 23rd, I was also contacted by Det. Maxwell with West Valley City Police. Det. Maxwell is working on the Susan Powell case and wanted to set up a meeting to review the cases together. At this time, the cases don't appear to be related. However, I will follow up with the information and review this lead further."

If you're familiar with the Susan Powell case, you might recall how Steve Powell attempted to link Susan Powell's disappearance to Steven's disappearance. Insinuating, the two may have run off together. In this narrative, you'll notice police rightly dismiss that notion.

Chapter 7: Interview with One Retired Detective

In September 2020, a telephonic interview was conducted between one retired Detective and investigator James Baker. The Detective states at the time, he was a homicide sergeant during the holiday season. He was approached by a Sexual Assault and Missing Persons detective, who asked this Detective to look at the Koecher case the sergeant evidently had. The Detective responded in dismay asking, why the hell has this thing just been sitting for two weeks; why isn't anybody doing anything with it?

He lamented how he was already behind after the car and laptop were released to the parents combined with the difficulty of getting St. George, Las Vegas Metro, and Henderson Police all reading from the same sheet of music. When J.B. tells the Detective the current property owner has sent him pictures of damage inside the casita. The Detective asks when those pictures were taken, since when he and his partner, at the time, visited the suspicious property, Sam DeMann allowed them inside both houses to look around. The Detective says that the damage was not there then. Mr. DeMann was cooperative; "he let us walk around the place," he says.

The Detective remarks how he felt after speaking with Mitch, saying "he was a squirrely dude, but we had nothing to tie him to the disappearance, other than just that gut feeling that there's something not right with that guy." Regarding the neighbor across the street, The Detective stated when he spoke to her, she stated, " if there's anything weird, it's because of 'that house,' and she would bet 'that house' is probably involved somehow."

He goes on to say he could not find any reason why Steven Koecher would be in Henderson. Interestingly, The Detective talks of Henderson PD responding to the initial call, involving a so-called abandoned vehicle, describing how he saw a moving truck there that night. "I could be wrong," but that's how I remember it," he says, after the parking enforcement people found the car and asked for police to come. The Detective asks James if he'd spoken with the private investigator who was assisting in the case. James says no, he's having a hard time finding him. (On a side note, he did locate this P.I., who told him that after 7 years, he destroyed any information he had collected on the case.) The Detective says this PI was a retired metro officer who attended the police academy with him, and they were friends.

In closing the interview, The Detective makes the remark of how Mitch DeMann could be one of those sons who's been in trouble so much over the years that Dad might ask, what did he do now? And he asks a poignant question here too. "The biggest piece of the puzzle for me was, why is Steven Koecher in Las Vegas in a Henderson retirement community? I never got the answer. Somebody's got to know why," he says. I think he's right, somebody does know.

Chapter 8:
Koecher Sightings

Around this time, "possible sightings" of Steven start coming to the police. One possible sighting occurred at a Best Buy and another one at a Home Depot. There was a report of a sighting at an IHOP. Some of the Koecher family visited this IHOP in hopes of finding Steven there. He never showed. Other sightings included a possible sighting on "Spencer near Flamingo, near the mall." Here is a sighting narrative directly from the report: "Caller advised that on 2/27/10 at approx. 1900 hours (7PM), a subject matching Koecher's description had been seen in the Sahara Casino with a white female. The caller stated that the subject had an Australian accent." Steven is from Texas, then Utah.

On April 10, 2010, at approximately 8AM, following a tip, a search was organized and executed by Steven's Father and a private investigator near the Henderson Executive Airport. The search consisted of nearly 80 volunteers, some of whom owned ATVs. The search yielded nothing of evidentiary value.

Now, this next police report narrative still fascinates me to this day. See if you find it odd too.

"On April 14, 2010, detectives received a call from a female who wished to remain anonymous concerning a possible location of Steven Koecher. The female stated that a friend of hers had seen Steven in the area of Las Vegas Blvd., south of St. Rose Parkway. The female stated that it was near the old Auto Auction place and near some heavy equipment and trees. Steven had bragged about being the guy on the milk carton (Anderson Dairy produced this in February). Steven was driving a maroon-colored Ford, 90's model, F-150 extended cab pickup truck with unknown plates. Steven was described as clean-cut, with shorter hair than on the milk carton picture. A few weeks ago, Steven said he was going to Big Bear, CA. for a barbeque but would be returning."

That narrative contains a whole lot of detailed information, doesn't it? Could it be; this is a misdirection? Someone throwing a lot of descriptors out there giving the appearance of some legitimacy? Or does this anonymous person simply know someone who looks like Steven? Sightings like this are not uncommon when investigating a missing person.

The same woman, who wished to remain anonymous, even led Henderson detectives to Sandy Valley to follow possible leads there. They report even illustrating how police visited "the only convenience store and bar in town asking employees if they recognized Koecher from the flier photograph." Nobody had seen or recognized Steven. Dead End Lead!

In April and May of 2010, some leads were followed up on

but went nowhere. Missing person cases are like that. Priorities are realigned. A whole variety of cases are created every day. Resources like personnel and money are stretched, law enforcement personnel retire, and interest wanes like a hurricane disaster one month after the event. The damage is still there, yet it is not talked about anymore. It's sad but true. Just another missing person whose face and physical description once graced the side of a milk carton and taped or stapled to so many bulletin boards, poles, windows, and buildings.

January 12, 2012, an entry is made in the case file by the lead Detective, "I ran Steven Koecher through TLO (a customized search and locate tool for law enforcement agents. Built on a foundation of hundreds of millions of records) to see if any entries have been made since his disappearance. There were no updates on driver's licenses nationwide, telephone numbers, arrest records, Email accounts, possible employers, or new addresses. The Case is continuing."

Just over one year later, on January 22, 2013, at 12:51:37, the lead Detective who worked the case and whom you've just read about, enters this in the report, "As of today, there are no further leads, and Steven has not shown up with any recent activities through our systems. Steven will remain listed in NCIC (National Crime Information Center) as a missing person, and this case will now be closed pending any further developments." This is where our findings come into play, and I believe there are further developments.

Chapter 9:
Exclusive Investigations

Exclusive Investigations was founded in 2008. It is owned, and managed by a man who we'll call Keith Winslet. K.W. is a retired police officer and former Detective, among his many other accolades.

If I remember correctly, there were only a handful of investigators at the time when I came on in 2017 as an "Apprentice Private Investigator." James Baker, the aforementioned retired F.A.A. investigator came on shortly after me. There were other apprentice investigators in our tight group, too; some included women. I've always believed there are times when a woman makes for a better investigator than a man does under certain circumstances. We all seemed to gel well, having coffee meetings on a regular basis to discuss and get updates on the cases Keith took in. Today Keith has approximately 17 investigators working with him.

As I mentioned in the beginning, James Baker knew the Koecher family in a roundabout way. On a very sad note, Steven's father had passed away about a year after Steven's disappearance. Words cannot provide much comfort for their loss, If there is anything that can be said to comfort the family, it is that Steven and his Father are together now for eternity.

Mrs. Koecher and other family members approached J.B. to ask him to look into the case. He accepted the task, and after I'd heard the case was in his hands, I straight away asked if I could assist in any way. At the time, he welcomed the assistance, and this is where I became immersed in the case. I've blamed him on more than one occasion for getting me involved. Today, I think he sees me more as a burr in his saddle, you might say. Well, it's his fault.

One of the first paths a private investigator might embark on in an investigation is securing police reports from the proper jurisdictions involved regarding the incident. Reading stories and viewing podcasts of the incident is another good resource for information. Using the Freedom of Information Act. J.B., being the lead investigator, applied for and received police reports from the Henderson police and the St. George police departments.

It's important to have both reports since Steven lived in St. George, UT., but disappeared in Henderson, NV. Once a case becomes a cold case, as Steven's did, records can be released using GRAMMA requests that are submitted to the proper authorities. In an open investigation, those records are not available so as to keep sensitive information out of a suspect's hands. In a typical police report there are narratives entered by the investigating officers. Many facts about a case can be gleaned from these narratives entered by police, such as dates and times, which can create a timeline designed to narrow down a victim's movements. It may also contain persons and their names, places, and evidence found or seized, as well as police investigative actions.

Victimology, as you recall, is a term used to study the victim. It can involve conducting interviews of associates close to Steven, i.e., Mr. and Mrs. Koecher, Steven's siblings, church members, friends, associates, and coworkers who were close to Steven. It can paint a picture of who Steven is. Studying his routines and demeanor prior to disappearing could lead to how he went missing.

During our investigation, voluntary interviews of persons of interest were conducted telephonically and in person by James and Keith. Both Henderson and St. George police reports disclosed names, times, and dates, all crucial in establishing events occurring in a chronological model in order to reveal patterns of behavior and movements. When a person's name is documented in a police report, background checks can and should be performed on those of interest in the report in order to get some context of the individuals who were near to Steven.

What is a background check, what does it consist of, and how is it carried out? The world we live in today is replete with information about each one of us. From court records to the already mentioned police reports, property records, birthdates, known addresses, phone numbers, associates, and even neighbors.

A lot of this information is termed "public information." Let's say you want to know who owns a particular home. The County Assessor's office is the place to find it. It's public information. If you simply Google someone's name, you may get some results of that person you Googled, or you may get results of someone who isn't that person at all but with the same or similar name. Facebook is one of those platforms overflowing with information about people, their family, their friends, their associates, their pets, where they work, how they play, the food they eat, and the places they travel to, just for starters.

I've always looked at Facebook as a kind of self-creation of one's own FBI dossier of sorts. The internet is a game changer for any investigator, offering up a myriad of data platforms that are more than ready to dispense almost any information you're looking for, for a price, of course.

Chapter 10:
The Landlord, Guns, Drugs, And A Stolen Porsche

While reviewing police reports, it's important to look at them with the same care an archeologist takes who sifts through the removed dirt looking for artifacts. This should also be a strategy when conducting interviews with any associates. Background checks ought to be performed on certain persons in the reports using one or two of the background check platforms available.

Combined with the police reports received, the background checks on some of the actors in this drama produced a cornucopia of criminal records, specifically B.B. and M.D. Clues and puzzle pieces are exposed, only needing to be fit into place. The landlord's background check, for example, produced a record of drug use, prescription drugs, many guns, and a stolen Porsche SUV in August 2009. Here are some excerpts from the actual police report regarding the stolen Porsche SUV.

NARRATIVE: INITIAL CONTACT: "Today, the complainant saw a 2005 Porsche SUV in his neighbor's garage. The complainant had never seen the vehicle before and asked why he never drove it. B.B. told him he could not afford to get insurance or register it. B.B. also did not have any plates on the vehicle. Around 01:15 hrs, the complainant saw B.B. pull into his home driving the Porsche, but this time it had a plate on it.

The complainant believes B.B. is trying to hide the vehicle for some reason. The complainant was advised to contact us again if he sees the vehicle leave again. Nothing further.

On 8-5-09, I received a voicemail from the complainant's wife. She said she had talked with the landlord and was told the Porsche had been parked there for 2 years if that made a difference in the case. Nothing further."

On 08/05/09, "I had dispatch conduct an offline BCI search with the Arizona DMV records to see if there were Porsche SUV vehicles currently listed as stolen in that state. I received an email on 08/06/09 at 1133 with two possible hits. A silver 2005 Porsche Cayenne was reported stolen on 04/26/05 by Phoenix Police Department. The police report number was 2305507031520000. The contact phone number was 602--------."

"By use of a flashlight, I ran the VIN number that I observed through the windshield. That VIN number was (redacted). Dispatch advised that NCIC was negative. I then asked Detective Dutson to try and Find a VIN number on another portion of the vehicle. I also asked dispatch to run this present VIN number through the Western states in an attempt to locate any possible vehicle registration.

While that was occurring, I observed an Arizona license plate that was on top of a workbench in front of this Porsche. I assumed that this could have been the license plate that was applied to the vehicle when the original complainant saw that the vehicle had been operated on the city streets. That license plate, AZ (redacted), returned to (redacted) Corp. out of

Virginia Beach, VA. It was issued to a 2006 Toyota Tundra. It is unknown how this plate ended up in the garage belonging to B.B.

Sgt. Long inspected the VIN after the initial check showed negative. He pulled out his knife and was able to peel up a small piece of paper with an altered VIN printed on it. This altered VIN, the one that I had observed, was actually covering the official VIN number for the vehicle. The official VIN was now (redacted). When this VIN was run in NCIC, it came back as the stolen 2005 Porsche Cayenne from the Porsche dealership in Scottsdale, AZ. This is the same vehicle that had been identified in the offline Arizona BCI search that had been conducted a day earlier. The stolen vehicle had been identified. The vehicle was unlocked. Officers examined the vehicle for any purposes of evidence collection; I noted that at this time, there was no license plate attached to the vehicle."

Four years later, as police are investigating B.B. for other offenses, this happens:

Sgt. Troy Beebe 10/09/2013 Initial information: "I assisted Det. Sorensen and Thomas, with an ongoing investigation concerning the sale and distribution of marijuana and prescription pills from B.B. In previous investigations involving B.B., investigators were informed by confidential informants that B.B. had several firearms and that he would carry a handgun in his waistband all the time when dealing with controlled substances.

Observations: 10/8/2013 at approximately 2230 hrs Det. Thomas and I were in the area of B.B.'s residence, actively looking for B.B. due to his truck not being at the residence for a couple of days. Det. Thomas and I looked at known drug houses in the area of B.B.s residence and observed B.B. leaving an address approximately two blocks away. Det. Thomas and I pulled in behind the vehicle and Identified that the truck was B.B.'s. The truck was traveling East on 205 North, approaching 400 West in Orem.

The driver, B.B., failed to signal turning South onto 400 West and then failed to signal turning East onto 170 North towards his residence. Det. Thomas turned on his red and blue lights. B.B. then accelerated Eastbound, pulling into his driveway, slamming on the brakes, and jumping out of his truck very quickly, giving the impression he was going to flee into his residence or attack pursuing Detectives. Det. Thomas and I yelled at B.B., "Police! Show me your hands," and then, "Get on the ground."

B.B. complied with orders. As B.B. went to the ground, I observed in his waistband an empty handgun holster. B.B. was detained by Det. Thomas. While walking towards B.B. (who was prone next to the open driver's door), I could smell the strong odor of burnt marijuana coming from the vehicle. Det. Thomas placed handcuffs on B.B. while I looked through the open driver's door to ensure there was no one else in the truck. I observed in plain view between the passenger and driver's seat the handle of a Glock handgun. I contacted Det. Sorensen and advised of the current situation. Det. Sorensen indicated that he would draft a warrant immediately. Det. Sorensen obtained an approved search warrant for the residence and vehicle. Det. Sorensen and Det. Thomas completed this investigation; for further info, refer to the Detective's reports. I assisted by entering items of evidence into Spillman. The items were cleared, sealed, and booked by Det. Sorensen and Thomas."

Chapter 11:
Background of Roommate J.Z.

The background checks of Steven's roommate Justin Zimmer, or J.Z., produced some small claim judgments against him, one even filed by the landlord himself for unpaid rent and reported damage caused by his dog. There was also a criminal class B misdemeanor conviction for "aiding a minor to violate curfew." Here is a synopsis of J.Z.'s record:

Synopsis of J.Z. Records

received 11-9-21

Criminal Court.

January 2008.

Case ending in # 01877

Aiding and abetting a minor to violate curfew.

Found Guilty, a $587 fine.

Small Claims Court.

June, July, November, and December 2009.

June 2009.

Quick Check for $1230.00

Case #00814

Check City

Unknown amount. Case # 00551. Unable to locate. Case closed.

July 2009

Easy Money Emg. for $634.44

Case # 00816

Liberty Lending $979.34

Case # 00911

November 2009

Nobile Finance for $562.66

Case # 01293

December 2009

Ridgeline Financial for $2869. 64

Case # 01135

The Landlord B.B. for $1953.78

January 2010

American Title Loan for $592.66

Case # 00057

Red Rock Financial for $2427.61

Case # 00104

Justin appears to me as more of a hustling trickster than anything. Or a deadbeat, finance game-playing fraud. I shouldn't be so mean, huh? He may have genuinely needed the money. He just couldn't or wouldn't pay it back. Offenses for drugs or domestic violence did not emerge in his background check, even though he was known to use Marijuana.

In a telephonic interview with J.B., Justin stated he had moved in a couple of months before Steven did. Then he moved out in October 2009. When J.Z. first moves in, B.B. tells J.Z. he will only be at the house once or twice a year. However, "in the first 6 months I lived there, he was there 3 times a week," J.Z. says. "We were not allowed access to the garage or his bedroom. But other than that, we had access to the whole house."

Justin continues telling James it was even in the rental agreement when we moved in that B.B. talks of only being at the home 1 or 2 times a year for business, and he needed someone to watch his vacation home. "That's what the ad said regarding renting it, but in the first 6 months of renting, he was there like 40 times," he says. "He would just show up at 1, 2, 3, 4 o'clock in the morning, and loud as hell, and I had to work." He describes in the interview how B.B. was in a different car every time and how he would frequently visit a place called "the strip" in Arizona. "He'd go out there and be there for like 1 or 2 days at a time. He was just an all-out weird dude," J.Z. says. Incidentally, "the strip" is located in Northern Arizona, bordering Utah and Nevada, just northeast of Overton, NV.

When James asks about the Porsche being in the garage in St. George, J.Z. tells him it was in the garage the whole time he lived there. Justin remarks how he should have known after the first day he moved in when he observed "like" 150 guns sprawled out all over the living room. When asked about a civil suit against him, Justin verifies B.B. sued him over his dog's damage to the carpet in the home.

J.Z. says he "just moved out because I didn't like who he (B.B.) was, like the way he was. I mean, he would just show up at all hours of the night. He was just weird," he says. J.Z. says he moved to Illinois and didn't even know about getting sued.

J.Z. says he didn't show up for court, and therefore B.B. won the judgment. When asked how J.Z. feels about the landlord's wife, J.Z. tells says, "I only met her a couple times; she's alright." When Justin is asked if B.B. had any people over with him, J.Z. says, "No, he was always by himself."

Chapter 12:
M.D.'s Background

More meaningful and quite intriguing as well, is the background check of Mitch DeMann, son of Sam DeMann, who police interviewed in February 2010 at the suspicious house. His background check unveiled several domestic violence charges involving at least two former female associates, girlfriends I suppose, as well as possession of controlled substances charges. These are big red flags waving here.

Here are two excerpts from actual police reports involving M.D., which were entered by Collier County, FL. Sheriff's office after responding to a call on August 9, 2003:

"On 08-09-03, at approximately 2141 hours, I was dispatched to reference a domestic disturbance. Upon arrival, I contacted the victim/reporter, identified as (redacted), who advised the following: (Redacted) and (redacted), identified by name as Mitch DeMann, have been having difficulties, and she moved out, trying to end the relationship.

DeMann had previously battered (victim) and had been arrested for domestic violence in the past. (Victim) stated that two days ago DeMann had grabbed her by the neck. (Victim) left the residence but did not contact law enforcement until this date. On this date, DeMann stated to (Victim) that if she went out to the bars, that he would give her "more of the same." (Victim) took these statements as a possible threat of violence. (Victim) contacted the sheriff's office for assistance.

DeMann fled the scene prior to our arrival. No injuries were observed on (Victim). I provided (Victim) with domestic violence brochures. No further information on the suspect's whereabouts was available. Thus, he was not contacted regarding this incident."

Here is another entry made by the same sheriff's office on August 30, 2003, after responding to another incident:

"On 8-3-03, I responded to (redacted) in reference to a battery. Upon arrival, I met with the victim. She stated that M.D., (the suspect), came over to her house tonight, and they began to argue. A short time later, the suspect, identified as Mitch DeMann, grabbed her by the waist and shook her. As she attempted to get away, he kicked her in the right leg, causing a small bruise. The victim and suspect have known each other for 3 ½ years; they do not live together at this time. The suspect had left the area prior to my arrival, and the victim could not provide a current address or phone number for him at this time. Photos were taken of the injury and placed into evidence. The victim filled out a sworn statement."

Chapter 13:
The Sleuth R.M.

In February 2019, a person reached out to James regarding some results of his own investigation of sorts. This person we will call R.M. for the sake of privacy. R.M. tells James he too is a person who has followed Steven's disappearance, and he would like to share what he has discovered. R.M. is, as near as we can tell, was the first person to make contact with the neighbor who lived very close to where Steven parked his car that day. After the two had corresponded via email a couple of times, a meeting was arranged where R.M. could be interviewed regarding his findings in March 2019.

We had no idea who R.M. was, or his involvement with the case. What J.B. was able to determine, is that R.M. is an over-the-road truck driver. The approach we took was to treat R.M. as a suspect. An old saying goes in law enforcement, "Everyone's a suspect until they're not." Guilty persons will sometimes interject themselves into an investigation to see where the case is going. Similar to an arsonist who watches the fire department fight the fire, the arsonist sets. For this reason, we planned on recording the interview as well as getting a DNA sample.

Before the day of the interview, we developed a plan where I would remain in my vehicle in the parking lot of the chosen venue to record R.M. coming into the parking area where we agreed to meet. The other people in our party would meet R.M. inside the venue. Once he arrived, I recorded him parking his vehicle then walking inside the agreed-upon venue. I then discretly drove over to and parked next to R.M.'s vehicle, where I would then get out and swab his driver's door handle with a buccal swab to collect any DNA, which may be on it.

I then parked my vehicle elsewhere and covertly entered the venue carrying a briefcase with my laptop in it. I would appear to be just another person having coffee and doing my own thing. I sat close enough to the meeting in order to record it on my cell phone, which I just propped up against my opened laptop and pressed record. I laugh about this story because as I was recording the meeting on my cell, I inadvertently had the flash on. A colleague, who was at the table with R.M., texted me, "Your flash is on!" Dang it! Turns out R.M. didn't even notice. Whew! I've made sure to not let that happen again.

During this meeting, R.M. told the group he was interested in the case. I believe R.M. said in his travels as a truck driver, he listened to podcasts regarding the Koecher disappearance. The case intrigued him to such an extent that he once visited the location in Henderson where Steven disappeared. And, on his own accord, he did some "knock and talks," as they are called, of his own. He tells the group that one of the doors he knocked on, a home very close to the location where Steven's empty car is found, a man answered the door.

After R.M. explains to this man why he is there, this man proceeds to tell R.M. about that day. He says that he'd heard a knock on his door or the doorbell ring. This man was in the restroom at the time, and it took him a bit of time for him to collect himself. Once he got to the door and opened it, he says he found Steven on the walk in front of his house. He asked

Steven if he could help him. Steven turned and said something to the effect of, "Do you need the money?" Something about money, he's certain of that. The man, not knowing what Steven was talking about, said no and watched Steven walk away.

This is a huge clue, in my opinion, and one in which the police missed. This is a witness who also puts Steven at that location, along with the now famous video. It also explains the six-minute gap from the time Steven is seen arriving in his car and going out of view, then walking into camera view 6 minutes later. Steven seems to have visited the wrong home at first, then after getting his bearings, he travels over to Evening lights. Could Steven have walked back to his car to verify an address he had been given?

A very interesting piece of information that should be noted here is, this house, to which Steven first approached, is the second house from the end of Savannah Springs Ave. The suspicious house, as I'm calling it, is the second house from the end of Evening Lights. Coincidence? I don't know, but it got my attention.

It was December 2019, ten years after Steven went missing. This anniversary weighed on me. The feeling of urgency was still upon me to get the case reopened. I recall a time I attended a coffee meeting that month with the team in a local coffee house. After the meeting was over and when the majority of the team left, I believe it was just Keith, James, and I who were still sitting there. Feeling a need to speak up, I seized the moment and took it upon myself to interject the fact that it was the 10-year anniversary of Steven's disappearance.

From my point of view, the case had definitely stalled, in most part due to police not actively investigating the case further. This was very frustrating to me because it had been 10 years, and I perceived individuals had been identified as persons of interest and they needed to be interviewed by police. It was my opinion that law enforcement somehow needed to be re-energized in order to do just that. I thought one way to do that was to contact an investigative journalist who could interview the police about the case and get it back into the public forum. J.B's position, on the other hand, was that we needed to bide our time as he worked with the Henderson police department. Based on the results up to that point, I lacked faith that the Henderson PD would investigate. Further, they were just stonewalling, and nothing was going to come of it.

But oh well, as a team player, I unenthusiastically agreed. That was my duty, after all. James was the lead investigator. I would abide by his request.

Chapter 14:
Armchair Detectives

I felt there was something I could indeed do, while dutifully biding my time and contributing further to the investigation. Websleuths is one of the places I ventured into. Websleuths is an internet true crime forum, where people can discover and read about many different types of criminal and missing person cases. As reported by Wikipedia, Websleuths was founded in 1999, and has over 136,000 participants as of 2018.

Websleuths members can make comments, exchange information, offer opinions, and for lack of a better term, become "armchair detectives." Each member can exchange information they've gleaned from their own investigation with each other. They can also share ideas, their theories and thoughts, of the many different cases in this forum. I don't mean to offend anyone here, because I became one of those armchair detectives myself. Some of you may know of Websleuths.

Websleuths has a section in it, specifically devoted to the Steven Koecher case. The participants in the forum offered up some exceptional and pertinent details about Steven. Many of whom actually knew Steven. I believe one member included Steven's cousin, and one included the landlord's wife, which to me, is rather intriguing. One sleuth even created a detailed timeline of Stevens movements around the time of his disappearance. I want to take my hat off to that industrious sleuth for their hard work. Thank you!

I must have read several hundred posts made by different sleuths on the site. Many posts I read were from the very beginning of Steven's disappearance. You see, as I've mentioned, it wouldn't be unusual for a guilty party to be participating in the forum in order to see where the case is going. Members use a different moniker for identification. No real names are used. I used my own moniker. An alias given to me by a man I met while employed by the local telecom company. I resented the name given to me at first, but grew to accept it as a term of endearment, and it stuck because it fit a work habit I had. I was always wearing gloves of one type or another while working. I revere that man to this day. My apologies, again, I digress.

As I read the posts in a chronological order, I began to notice a pattern of theories emerging. A lot of posts placed the landlord in a suspicious light. After all, he was the landlord who was owed money and the one with the checkered past now, wasn't he? Some sleuths believed Steven was on his way to a job interview that day. He was looking for work and in the video, he appeared to have a satchel or folder under his arm. They believed he probably had his resume inside it. Others believed Steven may have taken his own life after leaving his car and walking into the desert. And there were others who posted warm, heartfelt thoughts of Steven and his family. Expressions of love, hope, prayer and sadness.

Upon reading some posts on the site early into Steven's disappearance, in January 2010, it became clear to all sleuthing participants that one member, going by their moniker, happened to be the wife of the landlord. Mrs. B.B. a.k.a. T.B.

No doubt, when any attention or suspicion is placed upon a person, redirecting that attention is probably a natural thing to do. Who wants this type of unwanted attention thrust upon them? Please direct this attention elsewhere, please look over there, don't look *here*. Here are a few posts I found made by T.B., as she seems to point to some possible explanations of Steven's whereabouts:

January 14, 2010:

"I wonder if the police have confirmed where Steven's ex roommate was on the day he disappeared. J.Z. (ex roomy) moved in the night or when Steven was not home because Steven called my husband the next morning to ask us if we had been to the house, he was trying to figure out if our house had been broken into because some things were missing. J.Z. changed doorknobs and kept his room locked so he couldn't see if J's room was emptied. But the garbage can, toaster, coffee maker, and a whole bunch of cleaning items are the items I remember him telling my husband were missing. The T.V. was still there, so hubby told him his roomy had probably moved out and taken those things. This happened about the last week of October. My husband kept in contact with J.Z. and told him he still owed the rent and we didn't want to take him to court, but we could, and that he also stole things. J.Z. told my husband that we had no proof that he stole anything and my husband told him Steven had called us the day after he moved out, wondering if the house was broken into because things were missing. Steven was a witness that things were taken."

She continued, "When we finally did get the door to J.Z.'s

room to open, there was evidence that J had had drugs, and pot in his room. There were flakes and stuff all over the carpet which was not vacuumed, and on a shelf in the room, there was stuff out of a cigar and pot flakes, like the tobacco was taken out and pot put in. The cops came over to check out J's room and did see that stuff there. Other than that, the room was empty.

I keep wondering if Steven had found something out about J's illegal activities. J is pretty young, mid 20s, I think; but what if he was some kind of drug dealer or something?

I do not think Steven was involved in any kind of drug activity. I did not know him at all and only saw him probably twice, very briefly, the whole time he lived there; but he seemed like a shy but nice and easy going guy."

On the same day, in the same thread:

"The neighbor saw him/his car come home, stay for a very short amount of time and leave at 10:30 pm. It is possible he came back home again later that evening and left early the next morning, without the neighbors noticing.

If he didn't, he might have slept in his car, at a hostel, or with a friend. When my husband is on business trips, he will plan to sleep in his car a few nights to save on the hotel expense. I'm so sorry what your family is going through, we pray for you guys every day!! We just can't imagine what happened or where Steve is. He had been our best renter and we hoped to have him living at our home for a long time. My heart breaks for your family and I worry about Steven every day!"

Another post on the same thread:

"Has the family explored his Brazil (I think that is where I read he went on his mission) connections? I know his mission was years ago but my brother in law kept in touch with some of the families and people he taught in Mexico. If for some reason he did want to disappear intentionally that is one place he would know how to get around in and might think no one would look for him there. Could what he have been carrying have been plane tickets and a travel itinerary? How far is where he parked the car from the Henderson airport? I know that theory doesn't really fit the clues either but if the mission president there could put the word out, it couldn't hurt right?"

Another post:

"The house is a three bedroom two bath home. We kept the master bedroom/bath for us to use and rented out the other two bedrooms. The master bedroom has its own private entrance so when we did stay there we never ventured out into the rest of the house. While the guys kept it picked up they didn't keep the floors very clean and we have a baby. We were always visiting friends and family so if we were staying at the house it was mostly just for the night, then we were gone. Like I said I only ever saw Steven twice just in passing. Husband knew him better and saw him more than that because he travels a lot more for work and he took care of the renting the rooms and maintenance on the house."

"There were only two times I ever peeked into Stevens room. It was after he started trouble paying his rent and all I wanted to see was if his stuff was still there or if it was all gone.

The first time I quickly peeked in was when we stayed overnight at the house on our way to visit family, in Nov. His stuff was still there but looked kind of messy, the bed was not made and I noticed there were piles of stuff on the floor. In kind of a neat messy way like maybe he was sorting his laundry. The center of the floor was still clear. Like I said I was only looking to make sure he hadn't bailed out on us so I was just glancing in to make sure his stuff was still there. I would be hard pressed to actually say what was in the room besides his bed, desk, and dresser."

"The second time I peeked into his room was just before he went missing. We stayed at the house overnight and I think it was the Monday of the 14th. We were on our way back to Orem and I again just wanted to make sure he hadn't up and moved out. This time his room looked cleaned up. The bed was made and the piles were gone/put away. Things looked neat and tidy but it still looked like everything was there and he was still living there. I don't know if that means anything or not. I don't think it means anything too much because on any given day my house is a mess one day and cleaner the next."

And another:

"Sorry for the super long post! I've been trying to post for a few days but had to register and then wait forever for the mods to turn on my posting privilege! Yes, we know where J is and where he works. So do the police. The police have questioned J but I don't know how much detail. We have since heard rumors (from an Orem officer even!) that J was one of the biggest drug dealers in St. George!

If he was, it was not obvious, at least to us or he would have been evicted. Steven never said anything to my husband about Jordan and drugs either so I have no idea if or what Steven knew. Jordan did keep his room locked and when we finally got the room open there was evidence that drugs had been in his room. I do not think Steven is the type to knowingly participate in illegal activities. I do however think he, as many of you could be, given the right circumstances, was duped into something illegal, or a situation where he could be taken advantage of."

Post made by T.B on January 20, 2010:

"As I was falling asleep last night, after reading the passport was missing, I started wondering if there had been calls made to Henderson Taxi services. I haven't read anything about it but I haven't been able to read everything about this case."

And:

"I just talked to DH again. (DH was the term TB used for "Dear Husband.")

He feels horrible about the whole thing and said he feels guilty like maybe somehow it is his fault if it ends up that Steve left because of the bill situation. When I made the post in the last thread I was remembering a different convo DH had talked about having with Steve's mom.

DH had been calling Steve, and Steve had been answering his calls for months then around the very end of Nov Steve stopped answering his calls. In the first week of Dec Steve was now three months behind on rent and wasn't answering his phone anymore so that is when DH called Steve's parents' home phone.

No one answered so DH left a message that he was Steven's landlord and now Steven was three months behind and not answering his phone & he wondered if they knew what was going on. (like he was wondering if Steve was planning to move or something and hadn't told DH) That message was left between Dec 1st and 5th when his rent was due again." "Before DH talked to either parent Steve's dad called Steve to see what was up and what the message from his landlord was about. Steve's dad told DH that when he called Steve. He was shopping and he asked how things were going and Steve said fine. DH said his dad asked him about money and Steve said everything was fine. Then dad told him that the landlord had left them a message that Steve was three months behind. Steve was upset and said he wasn't THREE months behind. His dad said, well how much do you owe then? Steve replied it was about one thousand. His dad said, that sounds like about three months. His dad then said he heard Steve say something like, oh dad... as he took the phone away from his ear and hung up on him. I don't know if that helps at all but that call from Steve's dad to Steve was the day after they got the message. All within the first week of Dec."

Because some of the thread interactions I thought were so interesting, I included the conversations between the two members.

January 21, 2010

Comment: *"Don't feel bad unless you and DH buried Steve in the backyard. My landlord calls himself a capitalist with a heart he is trying to make money off his properties, but he will work with you to make it work for you...."*

T.B., a.k.a., Still Looking: "lol!! Kinda hard for him to catch the rent up then. That's DH, he was trying to work with Steve and Steve had paid a little bit, he had been paying some part of the utilities to help keep them on. And making promises and plans to catch up the rent."

Comment: "*You and your DH had a business relationship with Steven, and there's nothing wrong with asking a 30-year-old to respect that relationship. There's also nothing wrong with calling the reference listed on the lease. That's why there's no need to feel guilt.*"

Still Looking: "Thanks guys, that helps. I know we didn't do anything wrong but DH does have a big heart, too big sometimes. He keeps second guessing himself thinking maybe he should have called the parents sooner or handled things differently. He has been the one who has talked with Steve's parents and I know their grief tears him up."

I'm not sure how to interpret the posts made by Still Looking. One post in particular struck me though when she wondered of a connection to Brazil, after all Steven did serve a mission there. That very thought crossed my own mind in the beginning when I found myself wondering if Steven had escaped to Brazil. I even found Sacramento, Brazil. She seems to corroborate statements made by police in their reports regarding J.Z. too. Could there be clues in the words and phrases Still Looking uses? You can reach your own conclusion but, "making promises and plans to catch up the rent" could be one more clue in it all. In an upcoming transcribed interview with B.B., he does speak of a plan he and Steven made together regarding money owed. Back to Steven. I'd like to present to you a small sample of posts I found to illustrate how Steven Koecher affected many of those who knew him. There were copious posts from associates of Steven, all posting good experiences and thoughts of him, But I chose these.

A post made March 1, 2010:

"I'm a friend of Steven's. I met him while working a graveyard shift at the FedEx ground a few years ago. I just wanted to share a few things about him. I talked to him last before he moved to St. George. He is the nicest guy I know. He really couldn't hurt a soul. In fact, my mom recently reminded me that when I first met him that I was concerned for his safety because he seemed a bit naive to the evils of the world. He just finds the good in people and I felt someone could take advantage of him."

"He was one of my groomsmen. In fact, he arrived an hour late to the events even after I reminded him a number of times of the correct place and time. He is very smart but needs time to gather his thoughts. Sometimes he would be in the middle of a story and all of a sudden pause for up to twenty seconds. "I usually hung out with him one-on-one so we talked about deep subjects. We had similar situations since we both had degrees and worked crappy jobs. He seemed concerned in our conversations that he wouldn't be able to support a family even if he could find the right girl to marry. A year ago, I encouraged him to go back to school even if he had to live with his parents to afford it. He didn't like the idea at all. He seemed to not want to live with his parents nor go through the difficulty of school again."

"He is very tuned to spiritual matters. Within a year before he moved to St. George, he broke up with a girl because he felt God didn't want him to be with her. He was very troubled by it since she was just so perfect for him. During that time, he told me he thought he had already missed the chance to be with God's chosen girl for him. He had had the chance but didn't go for her when she was available. When he moved, it was sudden. I didn't get a chance to really say goodbye in person. While down in St. George I called and texted him a few times but never heard from him. I just figured he never got my texts because he complained once how his phone didn't get my texts."

"He is a great tennis player. I never beat him. He could hit a ball incredibly hard. He liked to play guitar and sing but I think he realized he wasn't good enough to make a career out of it. I am big into music and recording and he was a bit embarrassed to record. When we ate out he'd get meals of only a few bucks to save money. He once "splurged" and got an 8-dollar meal at a fast food place."

"Once we met at a restaurant and he parked his car down the block. I thought it was so strange. He said he had missed the turn. I couldn't understand why he didn't just make a U-turn since the street wasn't that busy. During a few conversations with him he expressed the conflict in his mind. He said at times he felt uneasy and anxious with his day-today activities. I remember him saying he was trying medication to help. It might have been a one-time experiment though. We'd always talk on the phone with a Russian accent. It was silly but it was fun. Steve is such an easy-going guy. He loved going to sporting games. He loved to do group activities."

A post made March 3, 2010:

"We worked together on the graveyard shift in summer 2005. I changed to the day shift that fall and he did the same around that time also. I think he quit before the end of 2005 but I can't remember. He was looking for the perfect girl for him. I think his regret was that he passed up on a relationship because she wasn't the prettiest girl. Later he realized it was a mistake to have not pursued her more. I don't know which girl he was referring to though. He broke up with a gal around the end of 2008 which seemed perfect for him. He told me she had everything he wanted. For some reason he thought it just wasn't right. God was telling him it wasn't right. I encouraged him to just continue the relationship and see what happened. However, he decided to end it anyway. His biggest sadness came from that event and the fact he felt he was being left behind. Most of his friends had gotten married and he was single and approaching 30. I remember him mentioning construction. It might have been after his FedEx job but I can't remember. He was pretty happy till 2008. That year is when he started mentioning these emotional conflicts. He had a good job at the Salt Lake Tribune but he wanted to quit for spiritual reasons. He said his coworkers were more worldly than he preferred. It hurt his spirituality for some reason. He knew it would affect him financially but it was worth it for his total well-being. That year seemed to be his loneliest too. Before then he had a regular group of friends but they had all moved on."

A post made March 3, 2010

"When I first heard he was missing; my first thought was that it was foul play. He never seemed suicidal or mentioned anything along those lines. He was a bit conflicted but it was only because I got him to open up. He was for the most part pretty happy. I sometimes lose my train of thought just like anyone can. Steve however when pausing wouldn't even recognize anything happened. If I were to lose my train of thought for such a long period, I'd joke saying "what was I talking about?". Steve never did that. He didn't look like his eyes were glazed over but just contemplating what to say. I got used to it but when he paused for the first time in front of my wife she laughed out loud since it was so unexpected."

A post made on March 3, 2010

"I'm LDS and I think it's quite weird to break up with someone for those reasons. I believe you should do everything you can and God does the 1% you can't do yourself. He wasn't a let God do everything for me kind of person. I remember him telling me how he applied to 40 jobs with no response. He was trying to improve his life. With that gal he had a persistent feeling it wasn't right. I think he was interpreting normal doubts of a relationship with God by telling him something. He was very in tune with his feelings and kept God in his heart."

"I recorded a song of his that seems to talk about the relationship with that gal. The lyrics talk about him being hopeful for a better day even though he hurts now. I didn't have a relationship longer than a month until I met my wife at 26. It's almost been four years since then. I just didn't need a relationship that wasn't going to be the "one". I think he was the same. He thought there was a special gal out there for him. The reason I mentioned earlier about his frugality with fast food was that he was also frugal with food the last few days before disappearing. His spending on gas was ridiculous but if he was thinking of ending it all wouldn't he have spent more blowing everything on food also. I saw him eat big meals. Three bucks at taco time isn't a filling meal."

A post made on March 4, 2010

"He said the pills he took helped him feel better. I assumed they were legal. I was shocked since he didn't seem like he needed them. I then learned through further conversations that he had a few issues. I think social activities and being around people were the best thing for him. Living alone for a while must have been lonely. Too much time alone concentrating on the negative isn't good for anyone. It sounds like he couldn't afford meds so if he did have any problems they weren't being treated. It might have affected his decision process. When I was single I went years without seeing a doctor or dentist."

"Quitting his job at the Salt Lake Tribune caused him a lot of money problems. His inner battle made him want to quit. I tried to convince him to not quit or at least wait till he had another job lined up. He tried to bear working there a few more days but couldn't take it.

I just know that he made some foolish decisions trying to better his situation. What that means in his disappearance I'm not sure. I'm just trying to let you know more about him. I've never met someone that stops like he does in the middle of a thought. It is just part of what makes him Steve. I'm also 100% sure it's him in that surveillance video.

No one else walks like that with that appearance. I know if I had his same money issues I wouldn't be feeling too well either. I don't know if the girl he was referring to in our past conversations was the girl he possibly was trying to visit. I thought he might have been referring to a girl that had gotten married. He was saying he had missed the chance as if there was nothing he could do."

"I just think it's interesting that he went to the temple one night and then drove more than a thousand miles over the next couple days. Knowing his history with decision making and his spiritual feelings. It makes me wonder. I always drove to his house and drove us places when hanging out since he didn't want to spend gas money. I know he travels a lot sometimes but if he does it must be for a purpose."

I read many, many posts from members who seemed to have genuinely known Steven. All of them describe him as a remarkable human being. My reasons for including the posts are twofold.

1) It is a reflection in the minds, and in the hearts from some of Steven's close associates of who Steven was. Some of their fond memories of Steven, the frustrations and regrets he felt, frustrations and regrets all of us feel

or have felt at times in our own lives. He was loved by many, and many provided love and support to Steven. As I said, it paints a picture of who Steven was and his relationship with his friends, his family, his co-workers, and his God.

2) In one post, there is mention of medication Steven may have been taking. It isn't clear however, what medication Steven was taking, or if Steven was using any medication at all. The point here is, "if" Steven was taking any medication, wouldn't he seem like a normal person as many of us are who take meds for depression? He could have recognized something about his mood was off and he sought help. According to the CDC, during 2015-2018, 13.2% of Americans aged 18 and over reported taking antidepressant medication in the past 30 days. The US population is roughly 300 million. If you do the math, 13.2% would mean approximately 39 million people took meds for depression during that time frame.

To anyone who reads this, anyone who may jump to the conclusion that Steven suffered from a mental illness, I say whoa!! No evidence has ever been introduced or produced, to support Steven having a mental illness. On the contrary, his actions, if true, may be a sign of good mental health after recognizing symptoms of depression and doing something about it.

Behind the scenes, while I am reading posts on this sleuth site regarding Steven, and monitoring it for further posts, James Baker is steadfastly requesting and receiving the police reports and accumulating background on persons of interest gleaned from them. This takes time; where weeks go by then turning into months, and now years. And, it should be noted this is not a full time endeavor for any one of us, but more of a, when I find time endeavor actually. All of the time spent on this case has been voluntary. Pro Bono if you will.

In order to collect as much information as I could on this case, I looked to the internet for more stories of Steven's disappearance. At first I simply Googled "Steven Koecher." I became somewhat amazed at all the pictures of Steven and the stories written about this case. I found all kinds of write ups which included many printed news stories, broadcast news stories, podcasts and theories regarding his behavior prior to and on the day he disappeared.

Here is one theory I found attempting to explain why Steven was there in Henderson: "Koecher's family believes, given his financial circumstances at the time, that he had gone to Henderson that morning for a job opportunity. Despite the odd location where he parked his car, in the video the neatly dressed Koecher is walking purposefully, suggesting he knew where he was going and what he was going there for. "He doesn't look confused or dazed," Steven's brother Dallin said in 2018.

It seemed all the write ups I could find included much of the already known story line about Steven and his disappearance i.e., his L.D.S. membership and the trip to Ruby Valley, the curious landlord and his shenanigans, the location of the empty car and speculation of a job interview there, along with the location Steven disappeared. One particular story I read even included descriptions of scars on Steven's body, including a birthmark forming, and looking like the Nike Swoosh. I thought a private matter like that would be more helpful to the police than anyone else. In addition, dozens of podcasts had been created telling much of this same story, but as is expected in a podcast, with more of a dramatic storytelling flair with background music and screenshots interwoven in it. It struck me that all the stories are indicative of a mysterious, intriguing and thought provoking account, all of which is true. The pessimistic side of me wondered if all these stories were just another type of news feeding frenzy regarding another missing person. An impersonal story to take up space on a blog or generate income for YouTubers and podcasters. All of the above is true, isn't it? And why not? If enough of Steven's story gets out into the public domain so much the better right? Nonetheless, all of the generated publicity as of yet, seems to have been fruitless.

Chapter 15:
A Tarot Card Reading

As far as psychics are concerned, you can call me a skeptic, yet even law enforcement has been known to use a psychic on occasion. I cannot say that I have ever heard of a psychic solving a crime, locating a missing person or pinpointing the whereabouts of a body. This may have occurred and I'd be very interested in hearing the circumstances of just such an occasion.

As James is performing his due diligence applying for and receiving records, I came across a Tarot Card reading somewhere regarding the case. Maybe from the Websleuth site, I just don't remember exactly where I found it. I thought it was through James since he did have a friend, or acquaintance who was a sensitive, or psychic, as it were. I do remember it though, reminding me of one of my favorite jokes, from one of my favorite comedians, Steven Wright. It goes like this, "I was up all night last night playing poker with Tarot cards, yeah, I got a full house and 4 people died." Ok, back on track now.

A Tarot card reader uses a pack of 78 illustrated cards and is divided into two sections, 22 cards major arcana and 56 minor arcana. Each card has a specific symbol on the card. The card reader turns over each Tarot card in a particular fashion and in a precise order; then interprets the card's symbol, as they are revealed with a particular insight to the reader. The following is a transcript of that reading I found.

Bear in mind the grammar and punctuation might be off a little:

The cover sheet begins with a quote by Steven's brother Dallin. It says, "The worst thing is that there are no answers," said Dallin Koecher, Steven's brother. "If we could find one little clue, if it just gives a little bit of closure, that would be great; or at least explain why he was there, what he was doing." On the cover sheet there is also this,

"Please note that Tarot will pick up TRENDS/VIBRATIONS of PAST, PRESENT AND FUTURE, it will pick up anything that is "out there," true news or false news. Either way it can throw light on what is "in the air." Please bear this in mind when you are reading the insights. It is very important that "readers" of the blog understand this, one has to be very discerning when reading. Media news can put out stories that are not factual or are premeditated, but Tarot can pick that up. It doesn't mean that Tarot is wrong, it shows Tarot can see what might be suggested. However, when writing the Tarot, it may be taken as fact."

Chapter 16:
The Reading, February 17, 2011

"There has been no news regarding Steven Koecher since he disappeared and very few answers. Tarot generally shows trends of past, present, and future but also does not supply all those answers so badly needed but, it might provide something that could assist. I write down exactly what I get in any given situation for a missing person and hope something might help. Tarot is not considered to be 100 percent accurate by law and for that reason you should always refer to factual sources."

"According to Tarot, Steven did go to seek a job. This card tells us that he was likely on his way towards a new job or a promotion. It is unlikely a promotion if he was having problems with work, which I understand he was. So, it looks right away that he had a message and a meeting scheduled for work. This card is North but could be Northeast."

"The number 11 may be significant in this card. This card also shows that he was walking, which all seems to fall in with events and it seems to me that this job could have been in the neighborhood OR a meetup. I am seeing a business here and there might be a dark haired female connected to it also a businessman. There are finances attached here so it might have been a position with better money prospects to provide more security and benefit. This is what it seems on the surface of the matter."

"There is nothing negative about this card that has been presented by Tarot about this day, or the intentions here, as this card is about hard work and goals of achievement. I am also seeing a school here or college and if Steven did not go to get on that day, this card tells us that he was going to study or go as an apprentice or "trial run?" It might just be an interview?"

"There seems to be a very diligent and determined element here. This card is also showing me travel, and is linked also to the Judgement card which can show health matters but also spiritual or church connotations. Number 21 could be significant and also some reference to 30 years, or 3. There seemed to be a bit of good luck here regarding messages and work? As I most certainly seem to see negotiations with work and financial matters and possibly even learning new skills. So it does all seem to point to a goal he had with someone and with travel in mind. That is what I think was happening when caught on camera which would also be shown by this card. It shows him with a purpose to go to a meeting with another. Soldiers could come up with this card and so can military, officers etc. Did he want to join the army? I have the word "Green " and see him at a "crossroads" whether that is symbolic of "crossroads of life" or whether it's a name or an actual crossroads, I'm not sure. What I do see is moving towards shelter food and a safe port in a storm, meaning, somewhere to go where he's provided for and it seems may have met up with an older man or older person and some link to the word "Hill."

"Sometimes caravans/mobile homes can come up in this

card, so I will just mention that. I feel as though it was a 'spur of the moment' decision and change of address/location with intent, and there appears to be companionship here so he would not have gone somewhere to be alone and had a destination and someone he was going to meet. Big decisions, living arrangements, business meetings all figure here as does being responsible and finding financial security. So that is what I seem to feel at first hand. I see rural land and flowers come up here."

"It's possible that with the female element, there may be a link to unhealthy associations-with the Devil card linked. It is only on this card that I see a possible problem. This would be between December 13 and January 9th. This can be connected to drugs or drinks or indeed it could actually be a very exciting, racy relationship or connection to a female and this could have created a huge change to Stevens life."

"I feel that if a female appeared here to do with work/business that he could have got tied up in this situation with her? The Queen of Pentacles is a good attraction card connected to Capricorn and work matters, so placing in the Devil seems to imply that he "might be linked to such a person as I am seeing hope and inspiration following this? Again a connection to the word HILL."

"It might be that a new job had elements that he was kept in the dark over. Not everything is clear here but I feel that there may be something to do with a female. I also see animals around possibly two dogs? The devil card can bring us into contact with either steamy relationships where we are really attracted to someone or it can be unhealthy in some elements but either way it does suggest we are "tied" to the situation or have bonded ourselves in some way."

"It can also mean a person is tied up but that is just giving all views of the situation. The main crux that I see is that Steven had a meeting and message to meet up with somebody male or female or even both, perhaps a female tied to another older boss? I do seem to see a rich man in these cards, but at first glance I don't see anything negative about that regardless of how it may turn out. The onward feeling of December 13 seemed to be positive and somewhere to go and somewhere to stay. There may have been an element of shock or a wakeup call to Steven. I'm seeing either a sign of a business or writing on a wall. The word Pan and /or Horn is shown on the Devil card."

"I also see either two towers or a Bridge and possibly some toxifcation (sic) of drugs/drink, or what I would call "poisonous water." There is also something about a "mother" here. I am wondering if he was involved or got involved with another female?"

"I could be wrong as there are many elements to the cards but I do see Travel very strongly and connected to the East or to the Sun. I cannot make a "story" of events and everything must be considered to be messages past, present, and future and therefore information is in "any order". I'm seeing a few illusions as though something might be known but not said."

"This card shows me a man in an office - someone who does not always want to be there. It also shows me a WEST direction but it is reversed and might mean Southwest though

I cannot be certain. Here we have an emotional environment around Steven but we might also take into account the watery elements too. This card is number 14 so all I have here is 1 and 4 to give us 5 or route 41 as route numbers or distance markers from "home."

"I seem to see the home is completely upside down. It's almost as though one cannot live there anymore? The separation is very strong and I wonder if I'm being given suicidal tendencies here because of situations that are too great to deal with. I am seeing an "insensitive" female who was not in tune or did not truly understand the situation, or how great the situation is/was."

"I am also seeing being cut off and cutting off contact in the page here and distresses in family life and feeling drained. There may be spiritual elements to this card because the 5 would link to the Hierophant and for some reason I am seeing Steven with someone else. There are Church values here both in the King of Cups and in the Hierophant which make me feel either a church connection is here or that he might be connected to the word church in a road name or even area."

"However, I can also see schools, spiritual organizations/mentors/ teachers and priests in this card. I am not sure why this has come up for location but perhaps he is connected to this in some way. Perhaps there is an "ex-clergyman" in this picture but I see something not exactly negative, but I'm seeing someone who goes against the grain here. Perhaps Steven just decided to stop being the good guy and go for what he wanted? The area to me seems like a water location or name of water and there is a red ship in this card which could have significance in some way, so I would have expected water/fisherman type names? Or religious connections. Stone altars can figure in this card and a strong connection to "drink." There might be some kind of deception here from a man-who hides his true nature, but I don't know who that is. Someone Steven met or felt would be helpful to him or whether it is Steven himself? The word "teacher" or "mentor" seems to be negatively 'aspected' here. I'm not sure if this helps or not."

"It has already been two years passed and this card has a two-year mention on it so I do feel there is a delay in finding Steven but I also feel he may be found by accident. I see him connected to a building-and for some reason the word "rubble." Perhaps he is discovered accidentally? He could have even had an accident. However, I see the word Hill once again and this may be significant. It feels to me as though he is somewhere he has been looked for already but not spotted perhaps? Because it's somewhere that is/was overlooked. I see a wall and flowers and possibly even a basement. The Tower card gives us 1 and 6 which is 7 or could be 91 or 16 all numbers that might be useful in routes or distances. Again the color RED comes up here. The 7 does relate once again to travel or some kind of property with wheels such as a mobile home. Not guaranteed as it may just signify travel on its own but frankly it is indicative that where he is has been overlooked as a possibility. The possibility of being linked abroad could also come up. As could hospitals, the Red Cross an inability to "heal" over something and some connection to the past. This is a very brief reading for Steven and I will look again in the next couple of months to see if anything else comes to me but will also come back and expand if I feel I have left anything out that I have not seen right away. I am quite sure that Tarot tries to provide some help and insight but not all details will apply though some may very well be useful." End of reading.

An Interpretation

Like I said earlier, I am more of a skeptic of psychics and even Tarot card readers, but as I read over this reading several times, I couldn't help but find interesting tidbits, coincidences, and parallels about the case. Remember, the reading we are told, can point to the past, the present and the future. So, as I read it over and over, I felt a sense of a mixture of all those tenses co-mingling together in it. Yes, I do suppose one could say the reading is vague enough to fit almost any given set of facts, including those facts in this case. And I admit, I don't know if the person who did the reading was briefed, or familiar with the details of the case, but it still struck me. As Joe Pesci exclaims in the movie JFK, "it's a mystery, wrapped in a riddle inside an enigma."

Let's look at some examples in this reading which I found to be interesting coincidences at minimum: The direction of north, or northeast is cited. As is documented, Steven is seen on video walking north and northeast as he walks out of view. And according to the cell phone records his phone pinged moving north days after he disappeared. On Google maps I found the North McCullough Wilderness, approximately 2.5 air miles southeast of Henderson. The number 11 is mentioned. It was 11:54 when Steven arrived in Savannah Springs. There is also an interstate 11 in Henderson which leads to Hoover Dam and Lake Mead. As far as "water" being in the reading, remember he parked on Savannah "Springs," and Lake Mead and Lake Las Vegas are not far away. The numbers 30 and 3 were also mentioned in the reading. Steven had just turned 30 on Nov. 1, 2009, and indeed he was reported to be 3 months behind in rent at the time. The reading also refers to soldiers or the army saying, "Soldiers could come up with this card and so can military, officers etc. Did he want to join the army?" The landlord does talk of his involvement with the defense department contractor BAE systems in an interview with Keith. How would the card reader know of this? The following statement made in the reading caught my attention too: "I seem to see the home is completely upside down. It's almost as though one cannot live there anymore?" James was able to obtain pictures from within the casita after this reading, from the current resident which show a lot of damage to doors and walls inside it. Looking at the pictures one could conclude someone was either mad as hell, or out of their minds, who then punched or kicked or used some form of implement to create so much damage. "One cannot live there anymore" seems accurate. I found the reference to searching for Steven alluring in this sentence; "Because it's somewhere that is/was overlooked. I see a wall and flowers and possibly even a basement."

And remember this interesting proclamation in the reading? "There may be spiritual elements to this card because the 5 would link to the Hierophant and for some reason I am seeing Steven with someone else. There are Church values here both in the King of Cups and in the Hierophant which make me feel either a church connection is here or that he might be connected to the word church in a road name or even area. However, I can also see schools, spiritual organizations/mentors/teachers and priests in this card. I am not sure why this has come up for location but perhaps he is connected to this in some way. Perhaps there is an "ex-clergyman" in this picture but I see something not exactly negative."

This almost sounds like the card reader knew of Steven's membership in the LDS Church doesn't it? Steven was a counselor under the supervision of GW, and no doubt Steven even held the Melchizedek Priesthood. I assume too, he would have authority to give blessings to those who requested one and or needed one. Furthermore, Steven attended two schools, BYU Idaho and the University of Utah. Remember, the Tarot includes past, present and future events in a reading. The reader's remarks about Steven possibly being found by accident intrigued me when coupled with these remarks made, "I see him connected to a building-and for some reason the word "rubble..." I have always believed the possibility does exist that Steven is buried on the suspicious property on Evening Lights. I believe too, that property should be sniffed out by a trained dog, and at minimum, be eliminated as a burial place.

The mention of "travel" over and over in this reading was intriguing to me too, since Steven had done a lot of traveling up to December 13. The word Green stood out from the reading. As I looked over Google maps of Henderson, I found communities with the word Green such as, Green Valley

North, Green Valley South and Green Valley Ranch. The word "Hill" is mentioned a couple of times, but what could that mean?

I will say this regarding the word hill, upon using the coordinates noted by police of the second call at 1053 hours on December 13. When I plugged them into Google Earth, it landed me on a hill in Hart, CA. That's kinda weird. In addition, I found a Seven Hills community, north of his last known location. There is also an Anthem Hills Park, north of his last known location too.

The reading also does hit upon "drugs and drink" too, doesn't it? The investigation found both of those same elements in the background checks of two people, Big Ben (B.B.) and Mitch DeMann (M.D.) as written about previously herein. "I see rural land and flowers come up here" is in the reading. Las Vegas and Henderson are both in the desert. Xeriscaping entered my mind as many, many homes are Xeriscaped there. Wouldn't the desert be considered a rural location? And in it live many types of wildflowers? The comments of a female are open to much interpretation, from the potential girlfriend in Ruby Valley, NV., to Steven's mother, or even B.B.'s wife, or, perhaps even a former girlfriend of M.D.'s. Lastly, when I was reviewing Google Maps, I found a place called Madeira Canyon Park about 3 miles from Stevens vanishing point. Madeira is an autonomous region of Portugal. An archipelago of 4 islands off the coast of Africa. Steven could speak Portuguese. No real connection I could see, just weird.

Covid

No-one will ever forget when in early 2020, we all had the unfortunate and a little bit of a frightening experience of being enveloped by the China Virus as was coined by some, later to be identified as Covid19. Most, if not all activity in this case ceased due to the lockdowns. In all the chaos surrounding Covid, it occurred to me that if I was going to be locked down at home, I was going to take it upon myself to learn a new skill. I'm going to put this time to good use and learn something, I thought. And I'm glad I did. It helped pass the time and channel my anxiety and the insanity.

As restrictions began to ease some, our team still had an occasional coffee meeting in places that decided to eventually open, but we were required to be masked, at least until it was time to take a drink of coffee.

Confirmation Bias

All of the police reports and background evidence which was assembled required careful reading, and deciphering. When I finally received copies of the Hederson and St. George police reports, I dug into them with the same enthusiasm as one of my dogs digging a hole in my flower beds. At the same time, Keith continued running his investigation business. James and I assisted Keith often by helping with surveillance or locating a person in the airport, then tailing their vehicle from the airport to their destination. We would also assist in placing GPS trackers on vehicles during the day or night. Keith had the cases if we wanted to work. Some cases are definitely more interesting than others, and some include humor filled stories that James or I could tell regarding surveillance, tailing, and tracker placement. For example, J.B. was once chased through a neighborhood by someone, at night, after attempting to place a tracker on their truck. One instance, as I was retrieving a tracker from a car, I was yelled at by a porch smoker who asked what I was doing under that car. I yelled back something along the lines of, I was asked to look at the suspension. "No you're not," she yelled back. Needless to say, I walked briskly back to my car and left in a hurry with all the lights out.

The information and materials gathered in an investigation are necessarily treated as "proprietary information," or the property of the investigator(s). Law enforcement keeps evidence they collect "close to the vest" during their investigation for good reasons. If pertinent information is leaked, or becomes known via someone's loose tongue, a guilty party could use it to their advantage. Moreover, leaked information could also damage a court case at trial. This is why we so often hear law enforcement decline to answer questions related to evidence. J.B. was keen on disseminating information he collected in a timely manner to Keith and me. I appreciated that greatly. Whatever information was sent to me, via email, text, or even word of mouth, I kept private and secure for similar reasons.

With a dose of causticity, I had an experience occur in February 2021, when an issue from out of left field, that I did not expect, would confront my integrity. As I've just spoken here of the importance of maintaining a "close to the vest" posture with sensitive information. Turns out, some sensitive information which had been disseminated to me and others, was leaked, and not by me.

As was our custom to have regular coffee meetings with everyone on occasion; a coffee meeting was scheduled close to my home. I did not always attend these meetings for different reasons, but this one I would attend. I like coffee and conversation and this meeting was close. I also enjoyed seeing and speaking with the others and hearing their stories as well. So on my way I went.

The coffee meeting started like every other coffee meeting I'd been to. Small talk, how is everybody handling Covid, some bantering among us, and the storytelling regarding interesting cases. The meeting began to wind down where most of the team had left. I had downed a sufficient amount of coffee causing the caffeine to swim in my veins with vigor. To my surprise, Keith and a colleague stood up and began to move away from James and me. The two both moved over to another table close by, for what I thought was to be a one-on-one personal conversation of some sort between the two. This left just James and me at the table.

James had brought his folder with him to the meeting. He seemed to always have a folder with him in our coffee meetings. He opened the folder and took out some paperwork and began asking me about a piece of information he'd sent to me. He was particular about pointing to a document code, or time stamp, or something with which he used to trace to me. He wondered what I might have done with this important document. In essence, and to my shock, he was accusing me of "leaking" this document. Befuddled as I was, and with the caffeine kicking in, I had no idea what the hell he was talking about. I assured him I did not leak anything, and that I would never do that. He pressed on, "yes but " it points to you, he said in more words than I can recall. He was convinced I had leaked something I had not leaked, and was determined to get me to admit it. I was furious but stayed somewhat calm, I think, except for the caffeine causing jitters. I knew I hadn't leaked anything.

Recognizing this was a big, big mistake, I again assured him it was not me and I suggested he look deeper into how this could have happened, and who else he may have shared this information with. I was certain if he did that, he would find the source of the leak. He agreed to look into the incident further and told me if he found out someone else had leaked it, he would have some "egg on his face," and make amends.

At the end of this encounter, I stood up, softly slammed my chair back into the table, and began walking away and toward Keith, seated a short distance away. While passing by Keith, I voiced the request, "can I have a word with you?" I met him outside in the parking lot. I again voiced my disdain over this debacle. I felt insulted and played by this plan of attack. "Why didn't you just come to me?" I asked. I would not be participating in any investigatory elements of the business until the truth of the leak was revealed, I said. One or two days following this event, I did receive an email from James. In the email he describes finding the source of the leak. It seems he had passed the same document onto a Koecher family member or an associate, who had shared it with another person. He admitted to the "egg on his face" and apologized. I was still somewhat furious and sent a scathing, perhaps over the top, self-righteous, and unnecessary email back to him. I would take that email back if I could.

I bring this up not to insult or defame anyone, rather to simply share a moment we all learned from. A teaching moment as they say. Somehow, sensitive information was leaked to individuals when it would have been better if it had not been. The point I want to make here and share with you is a term referred to as "confirmation bias." Confirmation bias, or tunnel vision as it is sometimes called, consists of evidence gathered by investigators which seems to point in a direction, or to a person the investigator believes could be guilty. Believing the circumstantial evidence to be enough and therefore moving toward arrest and conviction. It's happened before. Just take a look at the cases where persons are released from prison after many, many years, when new evidence comes along and exonerates them. As far as I'm concerned today, this moment is water under the bridge. A story to tell and laugh about at a much later date. A lesson we all learned from too.

Chapter 17:
A Time Out

The summer of 2021 was as smoky as one of my extinguished kitchen grease fires. Huge forest fires were raging in Montana and California, amongst other states, their smoke riding on the winds into Utah and enveloping its various valleys. In my view, it seemed prudent to shelter indoors as much as possible. It was one of the smokiest summers I could ever recall seeing in my lifetime. It reminded me of the huge sandstorms that form in the Sahara Desert, except it was forest fire smoke.

As if Covid and the smoke were not enough, in September 2021, one of my girls broke her leg. I have two retired, racing Greyhounds. Yes, I am a proud, reliable and responsible caretaker of my girls. One; had broken her right front leg after getting out of my yard through a gate I had mistakenly left open. Ugh! I felt awful! Just absolutely awful! I had already put one dog down on Father's Day 2019, and I remember how badly that one hurt, I was not going to go through that again at any cost. If you've ever had to put a loved pet to sleep, you know what I mean.

After trips to two hospitals, and a surgery, after a reaction to the anesthesia that almost killed her, and, after much money spent for all her care in a veterinary ICU, including a blood transfusion, lots of meds and home care, she is alive and well today, thank God! And I love her.

So, I took about a year off from life, hiding from the smoke, the Covid virus, and acting as a nursemaid for my convalescing loved one, helping her come back to life. And I'm glad I did. Even then, during the calm tims, there were times when the Koecher mystery still reverberated in the back of my mind. It did then and still does now.

How does the saying go? "If we can save just one person's life, is (fill in the cause) worth the time, effort and cost?" The same can be asked here, can solving just this one missing person case be worth the time, effort and cost?

Chapter 18:
7 Podcast Episodes

Meanwhile, behind the scenes, beginning in June, 2021, as I was taking some time off, James and Keith would forthrightly decide to go public and begin to produce, create and broadcast a series of podcasts of their own discussing the Koecher case. The last podcast to be recorded in September, 2021. All the episodes could quite possibly still be heard today. These podcasts included much of the evidence already gathered, including the names of persons of interest and the suspicious address. At the same time the episodes are being recorded, James was diligently looking for and finding, phoning and or sending emails to pertinent, important and intriguing actors in this case. Specifically, Justin Zimmer (J.Z.), Mitch Demann (M.D.), and Big Ben (B.B.), were all located. Several telephonic interviews were completed; one with the retired lead detective, one with J.Z. and three with M.D. B.B. would do a telephonic interview as well as an in person sit down interview with James and Keith. These interviews would be a big part of the subject matter in one or more of their podcast episodes.

Now, as I mentioned earlier, James and Keith wanted to keep all the information gathered private and secure. As well they should. I understood that and I would abide by that of course, but in the back of my mind, I always felt as though this case needed to be publicized again with the bright light of further developments and evidence shining on it. I was told these podcasts were put together in order to "get people talking." That could work too I felt. After all, the podcasts which were created described in considerable detail the case up to that point anyway. It's not uncommon after years have gone by, in any cold case, for people to talk after seeing a broadcast on T.V, seeing something on the internet, or hearing something in a podcast. It's also not uncommon for a person who knows something to come forward after seeing or hearing news about a cold case.

A person could be in jail, or prison for example, or facing charges and want to bargain with the knowledge or evidence they have for something in return. An example of stirring interest in a cold case involves the fabrication of playing cards with cold case photos on them. Then circulating the playing cards among a prison population in a particular prison, in hopes someone would recognize a face, or case, and want to talk. They could bargain with the knowledge the inmate may possess about a case from one of the playing cards.

Maybe playing cards wouldn't work in this case, but I wanted to somehow re-energize law enforcement by going public by enlisting the help of an investigative news agency and recording a broadcast hoping it would cause the same result. My colleagues were not of the same mindset.

They had their reasons, and good reasons too I guess. Nevertheless, now that the podcasts were made public, and contained much of the private information which was kept secure for so long, it no longer needed to be private. The particulars of this case were now out in the public domain. It was at that time when it occurred to me to reach out to investigative television news journalists. I did just that and emailed at least two investigative news organizations, one in Las Vegas, and one in Salt Lake City. I would not inform my colleagues of this endeavor to contact these two news organizations, until and unless I received some genuine interest back from either. I honestly felt as though it was time to go public at a deeper level, and I still do.

Chapter 19:
Interview with Sam DeMann, Mitch DeMann's Father

As you recall, in the interview with the retired lead detective. When he spoke of interviewing Mr. DeMann at the suspicious home and describing him as cooperative. How Mr. DeMann walked with detectives around the property inside and out. In the interview with Mr. DeMann, the story changes some. I do have to admit however, it could indeed be that Mr. DeMann is up in age now and may not remember the dates a younger person would recall with more precision. Or, is he distancing himself and his son from the time of Steven's disappearance? You decide.

I chose to transcribe this telephonic interview between James and Mr. DeMann for context and to compare it with the interviews of his son Mitch DeMann, and the interview with the then-lead detective on the case.

Transcribed telephonic interview with Sam DeMann in August 2020:

Sam: Hello?

J: Hi, is this Sam?

Sam: Who is this?

J: My name is James; I'm a private investigator in Salt Lake City, Utah.

Sam: Hold on a second, hold on... You're a private investigator for what?

J: I'm a private investigator in Salt Lake City, Utah, investigating the missing person Steven Koecher.

Sam: Never heard of him.

J: I'm sorry.

Sam: I've never heard of that name.

J: Okay...he...he went missing in December 2009, 10 years ago. He was last seen walking toward the house you used to own on Evening Lights.

Sam: Go ahead, I'm listening.

J: Okay...and on the day you moved out on December 13th, 2009, he was captured on video walking towards...ah...your house. And I think you have already left.

Sam: Wait...wait a minute, what video?

J: There was a video at the corner house on Savannah Springs and Evening Lights.

It was a mister, something like that. He was a retired Navy...ah...guy that was also an air marshal. He had a video on his house setup, and it...captured Steven driving his car into the circle...into the circle at the end of Savannah Springs, if I've got that street name right. And then 6 minutes later he was walking...it caught...it caught him walking down to your house on the right-hand side of the road. And that was back on December 13, 2009...and Steven... Steven's never been seen since then.

Sam: Why isn't the FBI involved? (good question)

J: Umm...well, there's no crime scene at this point...there is no....

Sam: But I'm saying, why do we have a private investigator looking for someone who disappeared 10 years ago when there should be the FBI doing this?

J: Well...they're not interested because there's not a...a... There's not a...not a crime scene. So my neighbor here was Steven's Aunt. So, I'm a federal agent. I retired...a year and a half ago, almost two years ago, I retired, and...

Sam: Uh-huh

J: Ah, my friend, my wife's friend, uh, I asked her for Steven's name 'cause I wanted, ya know, do some research and look up a new computer system we had, and that's where I got involved. We're actually doing this for free, were not charging the family, um...

Sam: Mmm-hmm

J: We just said we would look into all the interviews and everything that was out there and try and figure it out.

Sam: You know, it's kinda funny because this happened once before, around 2005.

J: Mmm-hmm

Sam: And the investigators came out and asked me if I knew anything, and I said no, I don't. Now you are telling me this happened in 2009? That makes it the second one on that same street.

J: Yeah, 2005, that's not; that wouldn't have been Steven.

Sam: Probably not; I don't have any idea. But ah...ah. You say they were walking to my house; when was this, 2009?

J: Yes, December 13th

Sam: I was not living in my house in 2009, so how does that come about?

J: Ahh...it was in a report that you guys had moved out that day.

Sam: *Chuckles*. Well, I think you'd better go back and check whoever told you that. I have not...I have not moved out of that house in 2009. I had not lived in that house until ah since 2006.

J: So you left in 2006?

Sam: That's right.

J: Hmmm...and who lived...did you rent it out?

Sam: I had the ...I had the house rented.

J: Okay.

Sam: I did not live there, so I don't under...I don't even know how you got my number. You wanna tell me that?

J: Well... There's...ah...programs out there called like, instacheck and ah...there just background information numbers and... that's...it...all our information is out there. I could run your background for you and send it to you if you're interested to see what's out there, but it's all public.

Sam: Yeah, I'd be interested in knowing that.

J: Okay. It's all...

Sam: You can text it to me.

J: Ahhh... it's a PDF. Umm, I don't think I...I can't text a PDF file ahh...

Sam: You can send it on messenger.

J: It's gonna... it's huge. It's probably going to be 90 to...most of them are between 90 and 140 pages long.

Sam: Really...

J: And a lot of it is junk; a lot of it is like neighbors, and ah, sometimes...it's not even...it's not even the right information; I mean...

Sam: Let me ask you something.

J: Sure

Sam: Are you the same person that called...ah...ah...woman by the name of (woman's name.)

J: (Woman's name) That sounds, that sounds familiar (woman's name) Ahh...

Sam: I don't know her last name, but (woman's name) was ah. She called me to let me know that the same scenario took place. I'm wondering if you're the same person...

J: Oh yeah, did she live in your house, or did she rent it?

That name...

Sam: She was staying in there with a person that I was renting it to, yeah.

J: Okay, yes. So that...so that was me, yes. That came up on one of the reports. Yeah.

Sam: Uh huh. Okay. That's weird, that's very weird. So whose fam...whose family was out there recording all this information?

J: Umm, his name was (air marshal name), and if you... it's on the corner of Savannah and Evening Lights, on the opposite side of your house. The other side of the street. It's a corner house. It's now owned.

Sam: Okay...And how--okay, and let me ask you because I'm kinda curious, how did you get that information?

J: Umm, well, that's on the internet of the video if you look it up...

Sam: The videos on the internet?

J: Yeah. If you look up Steven Koecher's missing person, the video, I mean it's, everybody, not everybody has it, but I mean, it was, it's public, it's out there. It's... it's a little bit grainy, ya know, cause ten years ago, our camera systems weren't like they are today. So it's a little bit grainy, but yeah, it's out there. I actually have the server; I was down there in 2019...ahh in December, my wife and I were down there doing follow-ups. And the guy that owns the house now had the server in his closet, and he gave it to us. We were having IT people, um, download the video off the hard drive to see what's there.

Sam: mmm-hmm, very interesting.

J: Yeah...it was his home...it was a home security system...

Sam: And that becomes (stammers), I say, and that becomes a public record?

J: Yeah, it's... it's...like on YouTube, and you know, people were supposedly trying to find Steven at the time, and so umm, it's out there.

Sam: And so he's never been found since then?

J: No sir, no sir.

Sam: How old is this man?

J: He was 30 years old then, so now he's 40; he would be 40 now.

Sam: I'll be darn. Very strange. And where are you located?

J: I'm in Salt Lake City, Utah.

Sam: Ahh, Utah, you did say that, yeah. Well, yeah, you can send it to me. I'd be curious to know how all this information came about.

J: Okay.

Sam: I have no knowledge, I had no knowledge of; this, Steven, doesn't make any sense.

J: Okay, now...

Sam: As I said, I had rented that home, ahh, it was rented,

and I had it rented for four years. So, I don't know how they connect me to living there. Doesn't make any sense. And the information you just gave me that I moved out when I did, when did you say I move out?

J: Ahh, they said it was December 13, 2009. There were moving trucks there. It was the same day Steven walked down there. One of the neighbors had told that to the police.

Sam: December 13th,

J: Correct, December 13, 2009.

Sam: Wild, that's pretty wild.

J: Yeah, now your son was living in the casita. Did he leave? Or do you know when he left the house or moved out?

Sam: The only one that was living in the casita was my son.

J: Right. Did he move out around the same time? Maybe it was him that was moving out.

Sam: Oh, I don't know when he moved out; I have no idea.

J: Okay.

Sam: I didn't keep up with that.

J: He what?

Sam: I did not keep up with when he moved out. I don't know.

J: Okay. Do you happen to have his number or anything? Maybe I could just call to see if he remembers ever seeing Steven.

Sam: He wouldn't know anything about it…nothing.

J: He wouldn't know? Okay.

Sam: No, he wouldn't know anything about it.

J: Okay.

Sam: Now you say he drove his car.

J: Yes

Sam: He was walking. You mentioned walking?

J: Well, he drove his car on Savannah Springs to the end of the cul-de-sac, and that's where he parked. And then he went to one of the neighbor's house and talked to a guy for a second, then he walked back in front of the cameras, down to your house, toward your house.

Sam: Wow! Wow.

J: So, in 2000, you think it was for sure 2005 that somebody else was talking about a missing person?

Sam: I bought my house in 2005; I don't know what the…I don't understand that. But ahh…

J: Well, I'd be interested in… I'll try and go through the records and see if there's another missing person back in 2005 on that street would be helpful.

Sam: Yeah, I find it very strange that you would think that they would have found him by now.

J: I know.

Sam: What about his car? He left his car there.

J: Yeah, he left the car there. Um, you guys have like an HOA...ah, security, like volunteer security people that drive around...

Sam: That's right.

J: And they saw it there for like three days, so they ah...ah...called it in...they got the plates, saw fliers inside the car, and...and called Steven's boss, and then that's how they got a hold of his mom and dad up here in Salt Lake, and his dad drove down with his (Steven's) brother...ah...

Sam: Ah...who was looking for him, father and mother?

J: Yeah. Well, actually, his father passed away about a year after Steven went missing. So his dad passed away about 2010-2011, but his mom and his family are still around here in this neighborhood here...

Sam: In Utah?

J: Yes, sir. I'm in Sandy, actually, which is right outside Salt Lake.

Sam: And they are still looking for him?

J: Yeah, yeah. And they hope, and then we get calls from, ya know, from the Henderson police now and then, when they find some remains somewhere, they'll call us and ask for dental records, or you know things like that, but, ah, they never, never, never found him.

Sam: No...it...that is... it's a horrible thing that he's (unintelligible.)

J: Yeah.

Sam: I think it's weird. I've seen and heard of people missing, and then they're found again but very strange. But if you could send me that information, I'd like to see it; I'm curious.

J: Sure, um, I don't think it's gonna come on text; it's so huge it would jam it. Do you have an email or something? I could just....

Sam: Yeah, I could give you an email.

J: Go ahead.

Sam: (email address)

J: Okay, so that's (email address)

Sam: That's correct.

J: Okay, it will take a few minutes for it to load into a PDF, and I can send it off to ya, and if you ever think of something that, um, that I'm missing or something, then I'd appreciate if ya...anything...

Sam: You'll include your name there, won't ya

J: Yeah, yeah, I will.

Sam: Give it to me again, please?

J: Ah. James Baker

Sam: James Baker. Okay, very good then.

J: Okay, Sam, thank you...

Sam: I wish I could help...I really wish I could help you. I'm in the dark, totally in the dark.

J: That's okay, I appreciate your time, and ah, I'll send this off so you can kinda see what's out there. Like I said, it's all public and may not be correct; maybe stuff on there, if there's another Sam DeMann, it'll confuse it.

Sam: I hope there's not another one.

End

I found it curious that Mr. DeMann immediately stated he had never heard of Steven Koecher. His recollection of owning the home seems to divert from the facts too. Remember, police state Mr. DeMann cooperated when detectives interviewed him on the suspicious property address? His tactic of insulating his son Mitch from any involvement comes out too when he states that he (M.D.) wouldn't know Steven, or anything about his disappearance either. And the one statement which caught my attention was when he said, "the only one living in that casita was my son." Adding too, he didn't know when his son Mitch moved out. "Oh, I don't know when he moved out, I have no idea. I didn't keep up with that," he said. Sam did seem quite interested in what is available about him didn't he? As he asks to have his own background forwarded to him.

Chapter 20:
Interview with MD

It's hard to find just the right words when talking about J.B. regarding his excellent work in looking for, and finding, certain persons of interest, keeping a case file, sharing information with Keith and me, in addition to keeping his head while working with me too. It goes without saying that all of us have the same preferable outcome in common; finding out what happened to Steven, and where he is located.

I had heard a relevant phrase some time ago, spoken to me by an old sage of a cop. He said, "Tenacity solves cases." A side effect of obsession I suppose could be tenacity. Jame's obsession paired with his tenacity, resulted in finding M.D. and getting him to voluntarily talk via telephone.

The following transcripts are of two telephonic interviews James conducted with Mitch DeMann. I have painstakingly listened to, and transcribed as best I could, word for word these interviews. The dates are accurate and so is the contents of the calls.

In June of 2021, James spoke telephonically with Mitch who agreed to be interviewed. The following is the transcript of their conversation:

M: Hello?

J: Hello, M?

M: Yeah

J: Yeah, this is James. How are you doin? Thanks for calling back; I'm sorry I missed your call.

M: No Problem, who, who are you with?

J: I'm a private investigator, and I was working for the Koecher family.

M: Okay.

J: And ah, we've been working on this for almost three years now. So, I am getting down to the end of things, and I wanted to talk to you about a few things if we could.

M: Sure

J: So, when you lived back on Evening Lights, do you remember when you moved out of there? The month and year? It appeared your mom and dad left, like, December...13.

M: Well, I used it. It was kind of a storage unit, slash, with a bed. I was kinda transient; I didn't really, wasn't really living there per se, I mean, cause I took jobs in other states.

J: Okay.

M: Um, the only reason I ended up in Las Vegas was because I got in a terrible car accident, and I had to have back surgery there, so I got stuck there. So, so, I was kinda in and out of there, and at that time, I wasn't even there. I was staying with a girlfriend because I was actually, I had surgery, and I think it was May 2010, and I think at that time, I was looking at the dates cause my Sister called me, notifying me of some internet shit with my name and this crap. And, so I looked at the date, and at that time, I wasn't even staying there.

J: Okay

M: Um, If I remember correctly, and, I was actually like paralyzed. I was stuck on the floor of my girlfriend's house, and I ended up being stuck for two weeks, stuck before I did the surgery. I really didn't want to do it. Um, but, yeah, I got in the accident, it was like October or November, and then it pro, my, like in 5 weeks, I really, my back really deteriorated badly. So, so, when I met with those cops there, I think it was before the surgery, if I remember and look at the dates correctly but, you know, I was on the Fentanyl patch, Roxicet. I was on so many drugs that, some days, I couldn't walk, somedays I was, I was functioning, and you couldn't tell, so it's hard for me to pinpoint the exact date. But at that point that he parked there, I don't think I was even there.

J: Okay, okay, so you had surgery in 2009 or 2010?

M: (sigh) ....my paperwork out here. Just so happens. It was 5.10.2010. (sounded surprised)

J: Okay...

M: When did he, when did he, when did he disappear? When did he park there?

J: December 13, 2009.

M: That's what I thought. So, ahh, Yeah, Um, So, I thought the guy, I did a little research, cause I was a little concerned, cause my name was floating around there.

J: *Chuckling*. Yeah, it's out there.

M: So, I'm not, what do you mean it's out there now? What's

going on now?

J: It's not now, but if you look back through all the shows and all the internet sleuths, things like that. Um, it comes out because he headed down toward your house; ah, Steven did.

M: Yeah, I know, of all the fucking, I know of all the places to park, right there. Anyway, so, I did a little research; one guy, one of the researcher, said that the landlord in Utah they were on drugs, so they were dealt...something about drugs, and he was doing some bad shit, and he went to Vegas, and I then thought they incarcerated the previous landlord that he owed money to.

J: Oh, he was arrested a couple, a few times, yeah, for drugs and other stuff, and we were in communication with a person that knows him, um, and emailing back and forth, so that's kinda slow right now. But, yeah, we, we, we, have been talking to him and trying to get information from him and what he knows and stuff like that. His name is B.B.

M: Hey, I, will, Hey, I, I, I, I can tell you this. I never planned on living in Vegas. My whole family retired there. That is one of the most dangerous places on the planet. Everything that happens, everything that happens in the Bible, still happens right there, the most corrupt situation I've ever seen. You know one side, the only people you can trust are the guys with badges, and at the same time, there's the corruption, its, its, it's an unbelievable deal. I've never had jobs where I worked next to pimps that had hooks, that, I've, I've never seen anything like it. I couldn't stand Las Vegas; I'll tell you that.

That is the biggest fucking shit hole I've ever seen in my

life. I haven't been there; my parents turned 80; just so you know, I haven't been there since 2014.

J: Okay

M: Yep, I can't stand that place. Um, and even just like this situation, for someone goes there, parks and disappears, just, just, ah, just discussed me. And um, um, I'll tell you what, I, I had nothing to do with nothing to that kid. But, I'll tell you what, if he went to Vegas and turned down one wrong street, that's all it would take. That's all it would take. I know for a fact cause I worked with the most prominent people in Las Vegas. I built, I built quarter million dollar aquariums or tanks, and I worked for those people. The richest of the rich there. And they built roads to deviate certain areas off D street, certain areas such as tourists unexpectedly will take a wrong turn, be smashed and grabbed, and killed immediately. So, and no one, no one wants you to know about that. But that is one of the most dangerous places on the earth to venture into. And that kid should have never gone there. And that's it. And I, I don't know if I'm ever going to go back. I'm not sure. I live in good old, I live in nice, wholesome Grand Forks, and it's a little bit different up here. You know, when I moved up here, the riffraff wasn't here. The gates did open; the riffraff is here now. But, still not like Vegas.

J: Right, yeah, it's a different world down there. Okay, um, I've got so much I still need to go through, um; I guess I didn't expect you to call back so fast, so do you mind if I call you again? Can I email you? How can I stay in touch with you so I come up with some questions? If something's not making sense, I can get your opinion on it.

M: You have my phone number.

J: Okay, alright, you work during the day, daytime, night time, is there a better time?

M: yeah, I, I, I work; if my hands are full and I can't get to the phone, I, I, just can't get it, I won't get it; I use my hands if you know what I mean, I'll do different things (stammers), but if, soon as I'm available, I'll, I'll answer it, if I'm not, I'll call you back.

J: Okay, alright, Mitch, I appreciate your time; um, like I said, I gotta go through a lot of notes here and write down a list of questions in terms of things I have and get back to ya.

M: No problem

J: Okay, thank you, sir.

M: Alright, have a good day. Good luck.

J: Thank you, bye-bye.

End

Nearly one month later to the day, on July 20, 2021, James again interviewed M.D. telephonically. The very beginning of this call was missed due to technical difficulties. The following is a transcript of that call:

M: (Technical difficulties). If you talk to (attorney name). He was my attorney there, okay. He may have the record. I may have been in the doctor's office on that day, umm, so, if the police would have probably done their job way back when, yes, my name wouldn't be trash, ya know I'm not; on one side, I don't give a shit because I don't, I don't have nothing to do with it. On the other side, yes, it's not good obviously if there are people talking shit, um, however, the reality is my, my movements were, were, ugh, they were so minimal there. They, like I said on that particular time, that I remember, cause I didn't have my, the medication right and I was really upset and that particular time of the year in December, I was, I was way messed up. When did he disappear?

J: Uhh, December 13th, on the day your mom and dad were moving out.

M: So, first of all, my mom and dad were not moving out on one day! They owned a house down the street for years. They bounced back and forth in this house for years. The van my old man used to run his shit and his plants and his tools, he did all sorts of stuff, so he was remodeling that house extensively, um, but I think he was finishing up at that time, I don't remember exactly, I was doing my own thing, and they were doing their own thing over there. But they were bouncing back and forth between there was definitely not one day! Anyone moved out.

J: The neighbor, see, these are the kinda things, I wanna kinda draw out the timeline, but the neighbor across the street said there was a white moving van, not the cargo van, the smaller van, up, at the house like 3 hours and that somebody was moving out fast. See, that's all these things...

M: well, no one, well no one was, no one, okay look, people who are moving out, maybe they're not screwing around, maybe he hired, maybe he hired a truck too, to move his furniture, which he would, ya know someone had to get a truck to move cause the van wasn't big enough.

J: Right

M: so, so a moving truck for 3 hours is not, that was not that big of a house. That's not that unrealistic at all.

Jim: So, these are kinda things that if you put an explanation to so we can help you, you know, put this to rest.

M: I don't have an explanation, I don't, I don't have an explanation, all I can do, is do my best to try, and like I said, my movements were so minimal that if we were to look back ten years ago, I might have been able to find out exactly where I was that day.

J: Right, well, you mentioned...

M: And I might not, I might not even have been in town, you know, I mean, who knows where I was, but you know, I did bounce around a little bit.

J: Right, now you mentioned (attorney name) was your attorney here?

M: Yeah, you know what, he, he would know he, hopefully, he still, he would have all the documents. And he, yes, I would get in contact with he's in Las Vegas

J: Oh, Las Vegas, okay; when you said here, I thought you meant here. Okay, Las Vegas.

M: Oh, I'm sorry, yep, yep. I meant I meant Las Vegas. Yeah, he's (attorney's name)

J: That was for the accident?

M: uh huh.

J: See, that's the kind of thing that I would love to be able to, a, um, you know, put to rest. And ah, you know, we're talking to the landlord, were trying to either get him to do either a voice…

M: So listen, let me, let, let, let me tell you this. I told you I was using that place as a storage unit kind of occasionally, but I really wasn't there at that point; at that point, I had a girlfriend, and I was really messed up, so I stayed for the most part with her. I remember I was stuck on her floor for two weeks at one point. SO, (very loud) the…ahh, man, there's so much I wanted to clue you in on. Then, the, um, lost my train of thought there.

J: That's okay.

M: Ah, ah, so, it was something about, mmm, anyway, the lady across the street. She really didn't like anybody. I mean, I guess she didn't like us. Oh, I don't know where the people are coming from. No one is a part in the watch cause all that shit is bullshit. I mean, no one even heard of that, and if there was any, you know, if there was any abnormal activity, of course, everyone would have reported that. I don't even know where these people came from; my parents weren't, they didn't, weren't paying members of the country club, so they weren't part of that club. So maybe that's where stuff came around, but there was never any loud music there. There was a guy that my parents rented that house to, and then he had a band; I mean, he had a band, he was in a band, and he had stuff going on. But

I never had even a radio there.

J: Right.

M: (unintelligible)...but anyway, there was something I wanted to point out that I don't remember now. (Attorney name) As I said, was good, he was a good source. He could be. Like I said, I don't know if he still has that info, and then, (Jim tries to speak) go ahead.

J: I was going to say I could touch base with him, but, um, I'd like to go back into the beginning. My, my folder's over 9 inches thick, so, umm, I guess I have a lot of different questions, and I would like you, just forgot your train of thought, that's why I don't wanna spend too much time on the phone, and you're driving and all that.

M: I just got to my, I just got to my destination.

J: Okay, even if you can just make up an email, I don't want something to ah, a good email you can answer if you can create one, and I can get my thoughts together, and you get your thoughts together, and we try to piece this together. Like I mentioned with B.B., we're trying to get him to do a voice analyzer or take a polygraph. It seems like he's gone a little quiet on me, so, umm.

M: Who's B.B.?

J: Ah, that's the landlord. Steven's landlord.

M: Okay, so

J: Without...this is the thing...

M: Hey...hey... so you're working fir...fir...for no money? I remember. I remember. I remember.

J: Yeah, pro bono.

M: So...work...your...really. Okay. So your other stuff, you're making money. You're just helping.

J: I'm a, I'm a retired federal agent, and I sell real estate, and we're moving, umm, and I do this P.I. stuff on the side just to keep me out of bars.

M: Okay. I remember my thought. Let me...let me...let me go with it a little bit...cause I'm more of a... I'm a talker... I'm not going to write you thru my email... I'm not. I don't... I'm more of a...of a..in-person-do-letters. I do formal letters. Don't like digital cross-dressing. So that's not my deal. So...so, okay. The deal with this, so I bounced around when I had...you know...When I had a reason to go there, I would go there if I didn't... I didn't go there for months anyway. I remember going there, and I remember the...the flier...so it said if anyone had anything to do...er...if anyone knew anything call...well, I didn't know anything about anything; I probably crumpled it up and threw it away immediately; I didn't know nothing... there's no one in that neighborhood that ever talked to anybody. It was a really isolated neighborhood, to begin with. The lady across the street, in particular, didn't like...I don't know...I don't know...who she didn't like, but she wasn't very friendly. So...actually, I think I tried to be nice. I think...I don't remember what happened, but she was actually rude to me. So, anyway. The flier probably got thrown away soon as I saw it...well, no...and the reason this is...you gotta understand Las

Vegas, going to the supermarket, you look on the wall, there's a hundred, two hundred ____ 8 to 10 missing people, I don't know if you've ever been to the grocery store in Las Vegas, have you?

J: Yeah, I used to live down in Mesquite... it's ah...

M: So, have you ever been, have you ever seen the wall of all the missing people?

J: I can imagine. I can imagine.

M: So...if... I'd never seen anything like it anywhere in the country, k... so, and I've lived around a little bit...so...you know you see missing people, and you stop and worried about all these people you'd be frustr...I mean, how can you do that?

J: Yeah, yeah.

M: So, the guys...the guy's thing on my door, I crumpled it, ya know...I didn't think twice. I crumpled it up... I threw it away immediately. And that was that. When I did make it around the next time, whenever I made it around again and I did see a card, I immediately contacted, so there was no delay, there was no stalling, there was none of that. As soon as I saw someone wanted to talk, I called and I...and I set up a date with those two Henderson guys...and...the detectives... and I met with them, and to tell you the truth it was creepy as hell because here I am, my back is killing me, I'm on enough drugs to make to this appointment with these guys, and just happens I'm not off my cane, and I'm blindsided a little bit because on one side you get used to these missing people, and it's just kinda like you don't think nothing of it until you've got two detectives standing in front of you and your just like woah..this is like..this is the real deal they actually think you could have something to do with this..and yes it's creepy as hell, and I was..it did make me a little nervous..so I was like what the fuck! You know, I can't believe I'm in this position.

J: Right

M: And...so...yeah...so that's an honest...ya know...my reaction to that. I didn't like it at all...and I gave 'em all the information I know...which I had, which was nothing, and, uh! That was that.

J: Mm-hmm.

M: And...you know, I don't know what to say, of course you're nervous when you, like shit, there's really a guy missing and...and...they gave me two people, they gave me this woman and this guy pictures...and...you know stupidly enough, when they gave me...the...the...the whatever...I forget his name, the boy's picture.

J: Steven

M: And...and...I looked at it, I said, I said it looks like he belongs in church, and ya know, I was just shootin' from the hip; I mean, that's what the picture looked like to me. He looked like the proper kid who belongs in church, and that's what I said, and all of a sudden, I forget what, they asked me about the Latter Day Saints.

J: Yeah, I do.

M: Yeah...yeah. And I didn't know the initials, and...I said no...and then they told me and I was like, oh, and I did; at that point, I said, well, Mitch, you better shut your fucking mouth because that just didn't look good. And just one thing like that, it freaked me out. I was nervous and only because...I...mean... they're serious, there's obviously a missing guy and, (chuckles) right on my street, it's the stupidest thing ever, ya know, I can't even believe it happened like that. But hey, ya know, I'll do whatever I can to help you, um, As I said, there are so many missing people there a day; it's not even funny, and it's a lot worse than Steven.

J: Okay

M: But, cause I think...I...think he was...I read enough about it, and I think he was involved in drugs in a bad way, and I think he ventured down there in a bad way, and I think he entered into territory that (emphasis added) he did NOT! He was not capable of entering into, because I'm from... I'm from New York, my parents are Italian, and I'm lucky to have made it out of there alive.

J: Mmm-hmm yeah...yeah, I could hear that in your dad's voice.

M: What do you mean, why...why in my dad's voice?

J: In New York, I think I could hear the accent. I'm from Chicago, so I could hear that Italian accent so...

M: Oh yeah, yeah my, my parents are both from Italy; they rode the boat to Ellis Island in the forties; they're just some stuff people.

J: Mm-hmm

M: And, they…they did not screw around. My old man put a paintbrush in my hand at five years old, and every tool after, and I worked and, you know, I'm still able to, you know, on one side, I don't talk to him too much, but I'm grateful that, I've always…he taught me all those talents.

J: Mm-hmm

M: Um, but, you know, as I said, I came from strong people, and I'm lucky to make it out of Vegas alive because I'm not… I'm not a shark; I don't… I didn't like it there at all. And to live in Vegas, you need to be (sighs); it's not, I mean, it's not for the timid or the weak.

J: Okay, well…

M: And I'm neither of those, but I just like to live my life like, well, you know me, man. well, you know…I got into some stupid stuff over there too,

J: yeah

M: And..and..and.. that's what happens too, you get, you quickly can..you can be in the wrong place really quick over there, and that's the reality of Vegas. Steven, the church guy, did not; he should have never gone over there cause who knows what he got himself into.

J: Right, so there's a big thing there, police officers and us, anybody in an investigation is confirmation bias, and we talk about that all the time. And, I don't know if you ever watched the movie ah, it's a Netflix movie, The Cecil Hotel, and it was on a missing person, and they let the story out to the sleuths and let the internet sleuths try to figure it out, and they convicted a guy that was at the hotel, a year before, and this guy, I don't like his music, he's dark, um it's not very good music, but he doesn't need to have

the punishment of ah this girl's death that he had nothing to do with. But that's the conformational bias, where you take stories, and you fit them together, and they fit your scenario. And that's what I wanna stop or prevent, and I think we could help you do that. And even if I could text you, er not text you, but if I could...ah regular mail you the questions I wanna go over, and I could have my copy in front of me, and you could have yours. And you'll have time to think about it and write down notes before we talk, and then I can do that from A to Z.

M: Yeah...yeah...yeah...yeah... that... that... that's fine too. Um...ahh...now I forgot what I wanted to tell you right there, but... Ohh...so...so as far as that goes, I already have, I'm going to contact, probably have to contact a couple of attorneys cause I already have a defamation suit; I'm sure I can win on these cases the cause of what they're writing so, I mean that whole girlfriend thing, (garbled) so I know exactly who she is, and I know exactly how, so this is going to be, it's probably going to be easy for the attorney, I'm just, there has to be a little exposure so I know, I figure it would let it cook a little bit...like I said, I'm not really worried about it, you know if they're going to come knock on my door, well...you know they...they...they can, you know if that's what they wanna do, but, you know, I don't think. I don't see...

J: Would you be, would you be willing to do a voice analysis and answer some questions, and then we would clear your name forever? The voice analysis is kinda like a polygraph, it just tells if you're telling the truth, and then you'll just be done with it.

M: The problem...the prob...well...I didn't...it...look...I didn't...I never even saw this guy ever in my life, so it doesn't matter. It's you, gu...know what I mean, you guys need to figure out what happened, where he ventured, and you already kinda know. There are people in there, I read about it, that know, that was right there, he knew all about it.

He said he got in trouble with that landlord, drugs, they were, they were...doi...and...and... I saw some pictures of him; you could see it in his eyes. It was clear as day. So I'm not concerned about clearing my name; I don't like what's happening; I may have to get an attorney and sue; I will do that, I will do that.

J: Right

M: And um ah, but the problem with voice analysis is my spectrum's all over. I bounce off walls. I'm 53.I got high energy...I only had one cup of coffee today, and It was early, and it's 2:48... and I still bounce off walls (garble). So...so. I'm just who I am...and when I got in one of those accidents, I actually did a twelve-hour neurological battery, and the doctor was amazed because someone coming from construction, said your vocabulary was that of a college graduate, and then my vocabulary, cause everything. I can answer a lot of stuff, and I had...I had...extreme ability...and he told me that my spectrum was one of the largest spectrums of a personality he's ever seen, so I'm not your average person. And the problem with this voice thing is if you can't hear me and ask me ques, and we can't figure it out, then I don't know what to tell ya. I don't... I'm not really a believer.

J: Okay

M: And all of the electricity...cause there are mistakes, and how is this going to clear? It's not going to clear me.

J: Okay, we'll do this... do you object to me calling (attorney's name) to see if I can check some dates? I'm not sure he will even talk to me; he may call you first. But to see...

M: I wouldn't have given you, I wouldn't have given you his number. If I would of object...that..like I said..if the cops woulda done their job ten years ago properly, I may have been able to figure out exactly where I was when the dude was walking thru that camera.

J: Right, right.

M: Aaa, so, ah. You know, I'm sorry they didn't do their business, and the thing is, like I said, there are so many people that, that go disappearing out of there, that shit they probably can't keep up.

J: No, no, they can't. And at the time, there, there was really no crime scene, and there's hardly anything to go on, there's no blood, there's no nothing, so, um, okay so, can we agree that it be okay to call (attorney name) um I'll look up his number.

M: Of course, of course.

J: And could I, I'll start crafting a letter to you, and I could mail it to you or whatever you want, texts, fax, um, I don't know if I'll text because it'll probably get jammed up, there's so many characters per text and it starts a sending new ones but, is there a way that you feel comfortable that I could send something, you have a P.O. box or anything like that?

M: Send it, and your, so.. you're not going to give out my address, are you?

Jim: No

M: You know my address should be public, I don't, I'm not hiding anything, I.. I've lived in the same apartment for 3 years, I pay the bi, I mean.I imagine all my stuff is already public.

J: So....North Dakota, I think, is the last one I saw.

M: Yeah, you could mail it to (street address).

J: (Reads back street address) Okay, I think that is the last one, 3rd St.

M: Apartment, apartment, apartment (apt. number)

J: Okay. Alright, M, let's...start... let's just...start with that. Let's see if I can find some good concrete, um, ya know, evidence in your favor that, um, shows there's no being in that area or whatever, ya know. Um, and in case you get a call from (attorney name), um, if you would…

M: So, hang on, hang on one second, you got your pen handy?

J: Yeah.

M: So, Dr. (Dr.'s name), k

M: K..um. You, you contact, you can contact them and, you can kinda, I tell ya, you should be able, him and I'll give you, I'll try and get other names, and (attorney name) and that Doctor, you start with those two, you should be able to build, oh, you know what, I got another Doctor, I gotta get...I tell ya, I gotta give ya this other guy, I gotta find, I wanna say (Doctor's name) um so I'll... I'll find his name; this is why I say this to you. When I finally could get myself to the...I got hit...you know my dad worked near the kid anyway, so my back was...I...I worked always, so my back already had issues.

J: Um...hm...

M: Then I got in a, in an extremely bad car crash, okay, actually I got in two of em. And I don't even know the sequence now because it was so long ago, and I went through so many pinpoint injections; the doctors took such advantage, it was so, I was so stupid it wasn't even funny. That's why I say one thing, I don't even know how I made it out of there alive.

J: Right

M: But, I let them do, like 9 pinpoint injections on my spine cause I had, I was really messed up. So, one of these accidents was the final straw, and that's at that point when this kid disappeared. So, that was, that was the fall of the year before when he disappeared. Oh, no, no, that year cause you said he went in December.

J: December 2009.

M: So yeah, yeah, so that's the same, ah, yeah, yeah, that's exactly the same time frame. So, between these doctors, I remember, ah, and then, we're gonna have to get all the doctor's appointments I was at because, I remember when I was at Dr. (Doctor's name), father-in-law, he was the neurologist that called me into his office cause I said I didn't wanna have back surgery, and Dr. (Doctor's name) father in law, who's another neuro, he's a neurologist that I went to, that I was at. And, he called me into his office, and he said M, and I said, I'm trying to avoid surgery, and he explained to me, he says you can absolutely not live like this, and he explained to me why. Ahh, so between those four people now, cause I remember going to the one doctor and he goes, well here's 3, 30 milligrams, he gave, he gives me a prescription 3, 30 milligrams of Roxicet.

J: Um-hmm

M: And he goes, here's enough here to stop your heart, as he hands me, as he hands me the scrip, well he was, he was giving me fair warning. He knew I was dying of pain.

J: Um…hmm…

M: But he, he, he, he, gave me this prescription because, and then shortly after that, I was on a Fentanyl patch, but, but, he gave me the prescription because he asked me how many of the Percocet, or whatever I was taking, and I said, I don't know you lose count after about 8 or 10, he goes, oh no.

So, and then I couldn't make it to his office, and then I did have someone, that, that a friend of mine, had these 30-milligram Roxicet, and I would break em in half, and cause I, cause I couldn't even get into a Dr's office. So by the time I got to a doctor's office, I was honest with them, and I said have you ever heard of Roxicet, and he goes of course. I said, well, I couldn't get here; I've been taking my friend's 30-milligram ones, haveI've been breaking me in half, and he goes, well, I'm going to keep you on that. And that's when he gave me the 3, 30s and he goes, here's enough to stop your heart. And he knew I was clever; he didn't want to see me die from this shit.

J: Right

M: But, but um, he knew I was dying, or he wouldn't give me this prescription. So, that, I mean, could have been the same day, ya know what I mean, I'm not sure what the, so between (attorneys name), (doctor's name), (another doctor's name), and this other guy if we can find his name who's a neurologist. Start putting together all my doctor's appointments, and I'll tell you what, I mean, I was in no condition to be doing anything, so I don't know what I would have been doing nothing with Steven.

J: Right. Okay, I'll work on that, but they're probably going to either call you or give me a form for me to send to you, and I can just mail it to ya. Because that's just personal information, they're not gonna, I can get with them and find out what their procedures are for that, and then I'll let you know, if that's okay, if that sounds alright.

M: Yeah, so then the other thing, too is, I don't have any of your credentials; I mean, I believe you, you seem like you're probably proper, but you're calling me; how are you calling me from a 218 number?

J: Oh, it, I got so many numbers, it's just a, um, a Rolodex, it just gives me a number.

M: Oh, okay, so I don't have your number? Or if I call this

number.

J: This, yeah, you can call this number. It comes to me. And a...

M: Oh, Yeah, yeah, yeah, it did.

J: it's 801 _ _ _

M: Okay, okay, okay, cause that's, see, that's my area code, and I was like, what's up, anyway, um

J: giggles

M: Anyway, ah, so anyway yeah, the only thing I really have is all those Dr. appointments, is my, is my thing there, and like I said, I've never eve, I assure you, I never saw the kid, and that's that.

J: That's, that's, that's what I'm going to run to then. That's what I'm going if I can; if I can, that's unproven, and that doesn't have to be you. If I can prove that you were just nowhere in sight or in the hospital or whatever, that's perfect. And we can put it to rest. It's not a, um, it's like this conformational bias; it just...

M: Ya know, that would be nice, and then you could actually end your energy and not waste time on someone that has nothing, you know what I mean, what a waste,

J: Right. Is there anyone on that block that you would be more concerned about if Steven was walking? Did you know anybody that, um,

M: You know, it was a really quiet neighborhood, you know,

I will ask you this, I will ask you this, and this is kinda curious to me. There was a gentleman that lived on, I don't know if it was the exact corner house or the one next to the corner house, directly across from where, or directly, I think he, see, I watched the video, I think he's walking on the left side, and if he hangs to the left, he's going to walk by this guy's house. Now, I saw this guy; I thought he was a detective only because I saw him with a sidearm one time.

J: Hmm, oh...oh, yeah.

M: And I thought, I thought, I thought, you know him?

J: Yeah, I think you're talking about, um, oh, I can't think of his name; he was an air marshal.

M: So he, so he was probably 55, 60 ish, and he was always, he was, I think I remember him walking his dog. He was one of the only friendly guys there. And, um, I remember he was friendly, and you know, I always liked to see friendly people, so I would always, ya know, say hi whatever, and he was, I think I remember he was walking his dog and, um, but I remember seeing him one time with a side arm and I thought, well that dude doesn't look like he'd be carrying unless he's a detective or a cop or something. I never saw him in uniform, none of that; I just saw him with a side arm one time. And he never walked with his gun on the street. It just so happens I was driving by, and he was getting out of his car.

J: Right. That was a, he was a retired military guy, and I believe he was also an air marshal, so he would never have a uniform on.

M: Okay, okay. So, so, have you talked to him?

J: Ah, unfortunately, I believe he's passed. He owned that house, that's the house that the video, cause he was kinda in security, so he had the video cameras that captured Steven, um, and I can't think of his name. We've tried to track him down, and I found a forum that has a family tree, and they believe that he wasn't part of the family tree, he just wasn't around when they were doing the family tree whatever, Facebook, but um, they couldn't find him either, and we believed he'd passed, and I found a death for his wife, um, a death certificate or a death notice on his wife, um, he had a weird name.

M: I don't recall ever seeing, shit ya know, it's been a while, ya know, and, and so you have been getting old too. So, but, I don't, I don't, I don't, ah recall ever seeing a woman there, but I just remember him, like I said, he's a nice guy, I'm sad that he's gone, dead.

J: I believe so, yeah

M: He didn't look that old.

J: Yeah

M: Anyway, anyway, um, so, so yeah, I, ya know, obviously I thought, ya know, I don't know why he would be a cop, but I know there was a cop or someone on the corner there so I thought that was, anyway (garbled)

J: Yeah, yeah

M: So, anyone else on the block, um.

J: Like past your house. The direction Steven would be walking?

M: You know, I never, I, ah. Ya know, believe it or not, I rarely even went that direction; I didn't have any reason (garbled) to weave my way in; I went up to my parent's place there and went back out the way that I came; I rarely went down that direction, I did a couple of times, but, but not much I mean, maybe only once or twice, I mean, I never saw anything out of the ordinary there that would stick out.

J: Okay, alright, you've given me a ton of stuff to work on, and let me, let me try to get some of it together, and if you get calls from the doctor's office, know that I was inquiring and uh, I can put a list of ah, items we need to put to bed and eliminate.

M: Yeah, and then you can send me your information

J: Sure, sure, absolutely.

M: Have a good day.

J: M, thank you for calling.

M: No problem.

J: Alright; bye, bye.

End

While I was chest deep in listening to, and tirelessly typing the words I was hearing through my earbuds, a characteristic of speaking became obvious to me that is not present in these transcriptions. This characteristic can only be heard, it cannot be read. Hearing someone speak is much different than seeing in print what the speaker is saying or has said.

A key element to note here is, one does not hear "inflection" nor the "cadence" in their speech from reading typed speech, or the "expression" they use in the words and phrases they are speaking, neither does it represent the mood, or state of mind the speaker is in when they are speaking. It's just funny shaped lines on a page or screen meant to convey meaning.

Listening to these conversations revealed to me at times all of the above. Small, hiding in plain sight clues, emerging from perhaps the subconscious of the interviewed participant, in this case it's Mitch DeMann, aka, M.D. His rhythm of speaking when he vacillates in and out of, or "'Bouncing all over" as he so eloquently describes himself, for me, was entertaining and disturbing at the same time. His choosing of the words and phrases he used, coupled with what one might call Freudian slips can be gleaned from listening closely to him speaking. These are all missed if one just hears and does not truly pay attention to what is being said, but really listens.

As I listened carefully to these interviews it became evident to me M.D. seems a bit scatterbrained to put it lightly. No judgment, just an observation. One of my takeaways from these interviews was how he seemed to want to control the conversation, steering it in different, unrelated and unnecessary directions, and interjecting irrelevant information. Could be indicative of M.D. just being himself. And, it could be M.D. projecting some kind of force field, deflecting probing questions too.

A third telephonic interview with Mitch DeMann, was conducted by James Baker and Keith Winslet on August 4, 2021. I did not transcribe this call word for word as I did with the prior two interviews, but rather made notes of interesting remarks he made in the interview. I also chose not to transcribe it due to the laboriousness of transcribing, coupled with the redundancy of the information M.D. has already shared in the prior interviews. Some of this interview I paraphrase and some I use actual verbiage.

The beginning of this interview starts as Mitch questions how James and Keith actually got his phone number. I'm paraphrasing here, but the question M.D. asked might have sounded something like this, So, so, so, how did you get my, how did you get my number? I'm not making fun of M.D. here, only attempting to illustrate his bizarre way of speaking.

The two men explain to Mitch, his number was obtained by a background check that included police reports of him. James makes it a point to tell M.D. he had made a call to him and left a message that was not returned, saying, "you never called me back." M.D. does not address Jame's remark but rather redirects to the series of questions he had sent to him surrounding his father, (recall in a previous interview James wanted to send M.D. some questions?) "I don't have those answers," M.D. says.

He describes his father as getting up in age and how he was doing his own thing at the time of the disappearance. His recollections of events, days and dates do not seem correct, he says of his father. M.D. starts in again with describing the "pin point injections" he was given and the amount of pain he was in. This sounds familiar doesn't it? A need to sidetrack, change the subject, bounce back and forth from the main theme of questioning to a side attraction of pin point injections.

In M.D.'s background reports are entries of the drugs M.D. had supposedly possessed. M.D. askes the two interviewers what his drug of choice was. Asking the question with a tone of, "if you guys are so smart, tell me what's my drug of choice?" James begins to look in the reports he has with him. He finds a police report that indicates M.D. was stopped by police and his vehicle was searched. Copious amounts of drugs were found in the car. M.D. puts the blame squarely on his girlfriend at the time, saying "she was mad at me and stalking me. She put those drugs there and called the police," he says.

Keith asks Mitch, if he had listened to their podcasts? He responds saying, "oh yeah, yeah." Keith introduces the notion of the different sides to every story. Telling M.D., "there is your side of the story, the other person's side of the story, and the truth story." M.D. does not comment on what Keith has said, but deflects again, changes direction again by pointing out a redacted phone number in a report he has with him or has seen before, "points to a lot of bullshit," he says.

In an effort to highlight his gentle side, M.D. pontificates how he does not hurt people, "that's not my cup of tea," he says. He then steers the conversation back onto Steven's landlord again, pointing out the landlord's record of possessing, what he calls, a homemade silencer for a pistol. "The only reason why someone has a silencer on a pistol is to kill people," he says.

The subject of a silencer has been talked about in previous podcasts. The suppressor along with many guns were seized by police after a search warrant was executed at B.B.s' home in St. George, which then became part of the landlord's record. Keith talks of all the conspiracy theories that are out there regarding M.D. and his involvement in this case. Keith tries to assure M.D. "if we can clear you and 'put it to bed' we will," he says. M.D. says he understands the need to find out what happened and wants to help. M.D. says (Girlfriend's name) set me up.

In his obvious police experience interrogation fashion, Keith changes the direction of the interview toward the Casita where Mitch lived. As M.D. has done before, he gets a little scatterbrained about being there at the time of Steven's disappearance. Saying at the time of the disappearance, "no I wasn't even there," yet he admits to living there several times in the prior interviews. His father, S.D., also tells police his son lived in the Casita during an interview with him.

Keith asks M.D. how the Casida came to be damaged, or destroyed as he calls it. M.D. states that happened prior to any disappearance, "yeah, I'll take the blame for that," he says. "Were you mad or pissed off?" Keith asks. M.D. responds back with, "honestly, that really wasnt me." He proceeds to disclose "the incredible amount of drugs he was on and how "the opiates make you extremely aggressive," he says. During this portion of the interview, M.D. describes his build as being 6 foot 2 inches tall and then about 205 lbs. So it really wasn't me, he says.

Steven Koecher was reported as 5 foot 10 inches tall and

180 lbs. This comment of, "it really wasn't me," could be interpreted as though he was out of his mind on opiates, insinuating perchance, that a sober me would not do such things. Keith asks Mitch if it was the result of a fight, or were you just on drugs and maybe a little paranoid and angry and in pain? "I was starving and on drugs, yeah it was a bad deal. It was really a bad part of my life," he says. In his odd method of speaking, he sidetracks again, and begins to babble on regarding the bodies resiliency to overcome such obstacles.

Keith, being the skilled interviewer he is, steers M.D. back to the time he supposedly moved out, or supposedly isn't staying there at different times. M.D. speaks of moving to California in 2007 for a while. "I don't have a perfect memory, I do the best I can," he says. He talks of moving back and forth a little bit. As is M.D.'s custom to redirect, he talks of the accident he got into in the fall of 2009. He continues talking of the wreck. He crashed his mustang into another vehicle, which of course, wasn't his fault. "That was the straw that broke the camel's back," he says. "I did some checking on myself, just to get up to speed and I saw it was on a Sunday Steven disappeared. "I wouldn't be at the doctor on a Sunday," he says.

"That was the time I was stuck on my girlfriend's floor. I was paralyzed. I was struggling to survive and that doesn't mean it eliminates me from being a suspect. I was trying to survive at that point," he says. James tries to clarify where M.D. spent the time with his girlfriend on the floor, "and that was in Henderson?" he asks. "Yep, yep," he says.

Mitch then asks, "have you guys talked to (girlfriends name)?" At that point in the investigation, attempts to find this girlfriend had been unsuccessful. However, a former girlfriend was found and interviewed via texting later.

The interview continues by asking M.D. if he had ever lived at a particular address that is read off to M.D. M.D. remarks, "That's curious too, cause I don't even know where that is," he says. And, you know what's puzzling is (sighs) there's an element that you guys missed, he says. He brings up another podcaster who has also followed this case. This Youtube podcaster has produced some interesting podcasts containing some of the same information and details we are detailing here. "That (podcaster's name) is overlooking a lot of shit," he says.

At one point M.D. calls the landlord "purely guilty and another road of possibilities." He climbs aboard another verbal train about the dangers of living in Las Vegas. How one could find themselves in the wrong place at the wrong time. "5 minutes off of a plane and you're dead in an hour," he says. He continues by rambling on about an old friend dying from using meth.

Keith inserts himself back into the conversation and stating he is not out to make any money (from the podcasts) but to simply get people talking and how we might get some closure for the (Koecher) family. "Your cooperation is truly very, very helpful. It helps clear your name and maybe even you being in the area." M.D. admits he's curious about the disappearance, albeit doubtful, unless someone comes forward and admits to it. "The landlord had a lot to do with it, that's your guy, and I'm willing to help cause I'm curious too," he says.

Keith tells Mitch how appreciative he is for helping get answers for the family. M.D. says, "I don't believe he started another life somewhere, but it's hard to say." Keith asks M.D. if he would like to go on one of the podcasts. In classic M.D. fashion, he says, "I'm going to talk to my lawyer and see what he says."

He continues by saying that he has looked into how he got here saying, "how the fuck did you get yourself in all this shit?" "How did you do that, when you had no intention of doing... no...that never."

Wow!! That was my literal reaction when I heard him say that. What is M.D. referring to? That is a very interesting statement all by itself. What shit is he referring to? How did you do what? Had no intention of doing what? Keith ought to be given much recognition and credit, as he demonstrated his expertise as a former detective in conducting this interview with Mitch; getting a response like that from him.

M.D. boasts of his "big project coming up," and remarking about changing names of his business or putting it into a trust and helping the community, "like I said, I'm not that worried about my own well being." "I'm pretty curious about what happened to this guy."

One other interesting comment made by M.D. in this interview is, "you know, I'm sort of obligated to talk to you otherwise I look like a suspect, you know I look like a suspect already," he says giggling. He then once more, like switching to a different railroad spur, begins giving a sermon about greed in society.

Keith continues to press M.D. in coming on the podcast, "...giving us your perspective and nailing down a timeline just a little bit more," he says. M.D. responds saying, "that's the problem, I don't really have a story do I?" "I mean, do I really have a story for this?" he asks. Keith points out, his living at the home and his criminal record does add suspicion, but it doesn't mean anything really. It's an opportunity to explain and give your account of the story. M.D. responds by saying, "you've looked at all my stuff." Keith reminds him of all the drugs he was on, suggesting he may have not been in his right mind during the time of the disappearance. "I was hyped up on opiates because of my injury and seeing doctors after the car accident," he says.

Keith attempts to put M.D. at ease as he tells him considering his background it might look bad, but there is another side to the story here, a human side. This could be why some of these things happened right?, he asks. M.D. replies, "yeah, yeah, yeah." You know my personality is, I'm a high strung Italian," he says. "I don't like taking any bullshit, and that's how I got myself in all that shit." (he giggles again.)

That is another interesting remark in my view. A high strung Italian, starving, and using who knows what, or the quantity of medications he was using, and who doesn't take any bullshit. What a recipe!

As the interview with M.D. begins to wind down, he boasts of how he carries a knife for protection in case he needs to defend himself from perceived stranger threats. He's afraid to carry a gun because he'd end up using it, he says. He talks of having friends in the U.S. Marshals Service and how he has participated with, and received combat training from them. "The guys with the badges, I feel I can trust." he says. In closing Keith asks once more if he would be interested in participating in a podcast whereupon, M.D. says, sure just let me speak to my lawyers first. Of course he does.

Chapter 21:
Interview with A Landlord

The telephonic interview with the landlord I did choose to transcribe. As laborious as it is, it needed to be done to understand better who B.B. is. This telephonic interview between Keith and B.B. was conducted sometime after the interview with M.D. In this interview B.B. speaks of a possible connection between himself and M.D. through "rock crawling" events. However, it is subtle and circumstantial. This B.B./M.D. connection is important in this case. The interview begins before the recording device is presumably on, or not yet connected.

Call begins:

B.B.: You know that he (J.Z.) and Steven were so different that they worked beautifully cause J was a partier. That's all I needed was another party in the house, where the parties got even bigger. J.Z. knew very little about me. I tried, 'cause you know I did come across as a high roller because I am a high roller (he says with some glee in his voice). I'm out having fun; this is what I do. I make...and you know...Miller MotorSports Park, the money I made throughout that...the other he didn't even mention, the federal indictment. I was federally indicted based on what happened on August 6, right?

Keith: The suppressor, or?

B.B.: Yeah, for the, for the suppressor, yeah. It was a class 3 felony weapons violation. Ah, because of the way the warrant was done. Ya know…because of ah…ah…ya know, this is where things get so crazy, but that Judge (name) dismissed that case.

Keith: um hmm

B.B.: It took two years to clear that up, so did you look at what I was dealing with during the time that Steven disappeared? I was federally indicted within days of his disappearance. My attorney called me at one point and said get all your guns and go visit grandma, and he hung up the phone, which meant you were under indictment; we had to arrange a surrender. I wasn't there when they raided my house and took the Porsche.

I was out on Lake Powell bobbin on the waves in my boat, thinking life's great. I got a call from a guy I was home teaching. I thought he wanted me to help him move a fridge or something. Ya know, he said that the whole block was surrounded by police, they raided your house, they took the car, they took all your guns, they set up a mobile command center in your driveway. I had really never seen trouble like that. I had no idea what was going on. No idea why any of it was happening. It took two years to sort it out. But that car is a big part of it.

Keith: Okay

B.B.: The other thing is if I was being federally indicted, I was working with the U.S. Army, um, I had…I had pictures disappear off my phone from like the Army intelligence; I took pictures of a crash scene that happened in October of 2009 that was out of Ft. Bliss.

Keith: uh huh

B.B.: Well, those pictures disappeared off my phone within days of me taking them.

Keith: Wow!

B.B.: I was in Las Vegas at the SEMA show, so I was obviously being watched by Army Intelligence federal agents by Utah County's major crimes task force. They just raided my house. They took a Porsche, which was a $115,000 car in absolutely perfect condition even after three years; my job there was to store and maintain that car just like I did with the 6-wheel drive Mercedes just like I did my own fleet of cars. I had multiple garages and places to keep things.

Keith: um, hum, so are you going to be in...are you in Salt Lake?

B.B.: No, but... I'll be...probably as far north as Utah County by the end of the week.

Keith: I mean, James and I would; I mean, we...we'll, ya know, we'll sit down with you. I mean, that's not a problem; I mean...like to hear your story, right?

B.B.: I would like to especially...yeah a the....

Keith: ...is all about...is... I can tell you James is a neighbor to Steven's family, and we took this case on; we were actually retained by the family to try and get information. It's not some podcast; it's not some T.V. show that showcases him. We're actually trying to find answers for the family and to weed out people who aren't involved and... and. I don't think you're involved, but let's talk about it and clear the air, right?

B.B.: Well, then I got the emails that were sent to my brother, and so I understand all that, but you gotta understand why you speak...take into account that...that Porsche was part of a larger picture and that other people were killed over evidence and for turning evidence against this group.

Keith: Sure. I got you.

B.B.: So, do you think it is possible that somebody said, you know, that Steven was mixed up in that? That he was disappeared...

Keith: Certainly possible, right? Um...I mean, anything's possible and.

B.B.: And so I'd like to get to the bottom of it too. The way you're looking at me and my life is like totally different, and yet my criminal record, you pretty much got most of it, but you gotta consider August 6, my house is raided... I'm. I'm charged, so I arranged a surrender three days later, I'm. I'm booked and released, and then I'm indicted.

Keith: Uh huh.

B.B.: And after I'm indicted, I'm booked and released to a pre-trial probation officer, so the reason the police never questioned me, I was never a suspect. They knew where I was the whole time. They had a lot of different people watching me throughout that time.

Keith: Well, and you probably, I mean, if you were under indictment, you weren't talking to anybody anyway, you know what I mean?

B.B.: Well, and the other thing, the other thing to take into account is...you know, I'm a fellow member of the church with Steven, and I didn't have a whole lot of love for Justin. He was... you know, he was the partyer who snuck out the window in the middle of the night. But Steven called me that next morning, and he said, ahh...were you here last night? And I said no, I'm in Orem. And he said well, the house has been cleared out, and Justin's gone. And I said, well, ya know, call the police will, Well, make a report on it.

Keith: Um, hmm

B.B.: And so we did. We reported it. Then...so I had a criminal case and a civil case against Justin, which I don't... he's a mouth breather; he's not smart enough to instigate anything, but... ya know...there...there...it could be...ya know, I'm not going to rule anything out.

Keith: Sure, well that's kinda what we're doing is, we don't want to rule anything out, but if we can talk...

B.B.: But I don't think...I really don't think Justin was involved, and I never really did, and some of the information my wife was putting out was coming directly from the Koecher family at the time like the information about some cops saying that Justin was the biggest drug dealer in St. George, like that came through the Koecher family if I remember right. Like somebody...somebody on that...or...or through some other information

Keith: Okay

B.B.: Cause they...you know...the other thing is. The Koecher family. I don't know how they reacted to it. But when I called Steven's dad, it was out of concern for Steven, not the rent, the rent was a concern, but Steven had made...he...the deal we had made together was that he was moving out. He was going to go on somewhere else; he acknowledged that he owed me the money, he was willing to pay it with no problem, and I was willing to accept it no problem whenever. That was the deal. That the money...was...it was...the debt wasn't going to get any bigger. He acknowledged it and was willing to pay for it; that's all I needed from him. His word was as good as signed in blood, right?

Keith: Right

B.B.: So I had also found a letter that I had written, and it was... probably to my attorney, but it mentioned the St. George house and that I had renters there that hadn't...neither one had paid rent since October, is what I wrote, but I would be able to re-rent the house after the first of the year. And it was dated September 10. So, I don't remember the specifics exactly, but I remember spending a lot of time in person with Steven right there in front of the house, and he was asking me about how I lived and how I traveled all over and went where I wanted when I want, ya know, how I want and we had some really good discussions, and I was telling him, ya know your young, you're single, you can do whatever you want, whenever, wherever like ya know...

Keith: Yeah

B.B.: And I wasn't rushing him to move out of the house

because he was taking good care of the place. I wanted him there in a way so Justin wasn't there alone.

Keith: Yeah

B.B.: I mean, in a way, he was helping protect an asset. And when you're looking at $1500. Miller MotorSports Park gave me a quarter million. I...you know...the money wasn't the issue. At that point, I was pretty tight on money 'cause I was paying attorneys and everything else. That was when my world fell apart.

Keith: Right

B.B.: But the other thing was ...ah...the...case wasn't closed until August 2011. And that's when I paid that $5000.00 restitution on the car. They gave me all my guns back, everything was good, and then, like a month later, they hit me again. So, I was raided five times in 10 years...er...no... I was raided ten times in 5 years.

Keith: Wow.

B.B.: Between traffic stops and then hitting me at the house. The other thing you couldn't figure out, a judge saying you got a word for word, you heard it, you read it,

Keith: I read it...

B.B.: You've got 48 hours to get out of this state.

Keith: Which I would like....

B.B.: You think there's more to it...

Keith: That happened, right?

B.B.: That's his way of saying, "Run!"

Keith: Yeah

B.B.: They're never going to leave you alone; run. And the ankle monitor was to prove as court-admissible evidence; they couldn't come back and say hey, you came back to Utah. I had no further restrictions. Like the guy that was monitoring me watched me drive to L.A. and back to Phoenix and all. He's like, you just covered. You know you didn't go back to Utah, but you covered 1500 miles in the last couple of days, ya know.

Keith: Mmm hmm.

B.B.: He was laughing at me, like, and I paid him cash, $10 a day for that monitoring time. And it was court-admissible evidence that I didn't go back to Utah and that. Cause…that…that major crimes task force, they weren't going to leave me alone. That night, they were there with masks over their faces; they had fully automatic weapons. They took everything I owned, as far as guns and everything, with no warrant that night. It was a traffic stop they executed in my driveway. Remember how they mentioned I took off?

Keith: Umm hmm.

B.B.: They were in unmarked cars and plain clothes, and I just dropped off my personal assistant, who was the confidential informant that's the house they were watching because he was talking to them. As I dropped him off, I went around the corner; 3 of them surrounded me, and..and..my personal assistant talked me into going up into a place where I had a bunch of guns stashed for a rainy day fund so I could move out of the state. He talked me into getting those guns and bringing them down in town. I dropped..he had me drop. I was like...just walk home. He had me drop him off first; he left paraphernalia in plain sight as he got out of the truck. Within..within 5 seconds, they were on me, and I...but it was half a block from the house. So I got three cars surrounding me that are unmarked, and I've got a truck full of guns. When I jumped out of my truck, I had a Glock in each hand; I thought it was a hit. I pulled up where I thought I had a defensive position.

Keith: Umm...hmm...

B.B.: And the second I figured out they were cops, I surrendered my guns. And I surrendered myself. When I realized they were cops, that's when I surrendered; no problem; you can look at my record. There's never been a failure to appear.

Keith: No, we looked at that right; I mean, we actually...

B.B.: There's never been a victim, there's never been a violent crime; I mean, other than the insurance company, and that Porsche is a different deal...and... the furniture store deal, that was another thing that is like, ya know before I knew about the law before I knew they couldn't just push me around like that...

Keith: Umm hmm.

B.B.: Before I knew people, ya know, were going to get away with lying about me. But you look at five different different snitches, all those charges, all that chaos; why did they want me so bad? And then that night, when.. when they...you know, the plainclothes cops, and then 20 cops are standing in my kitchen. They brought all my guns, and there wasn't a single gun in the house; there weren't any drugs in the house. It was a big house with a detached garage. Everything they found was in the garage or the truck. The next morning...this is interesting. Have you got a second for this story?

Keith: Sure, what's up?

B.B.: Okay, so that night, as I pulled in my driveway, they didn't have a warrant; they lied to my wife to get her to answer the door, they searched the house, and ah...they didn't find anything in the house, but they went out to my office in the garage, and they brought all my guns out and piled them up on the kitchen table, and one of those cops looked at me while Im in handcuffs, and said this is a lot of money worth of guns. Aren't you worried about someone breaking in here and stealing 'em? And all the other cops started laughing at him, and I said what the hell do you think is happening to me right now? And he said, Oh, you think we're stealing 'em. And I never did get 'em back. And so when I was raised, I was taught, you know, you have a second amendment, right? you have the right to self-protection.

Keith: Right

B.B.: And then I was also taught about this free country. Have you ever gone to a doctor? This is for you personally, Kevin. Have you gone to a doctor, and...has the doctor ever written you a prescription?

Keith: Sure.

B.B.: And did you fill that prescription and take it?

Keith: Sure.

B.B.: That's what I did with marijuana. And so, to accuse me of having a drug problem, I have never once abused prescription medication. I have never had a drug problem. I have had a problem with people…there are two types of people in the world, right? Those who wanna be left alone, and those who won't leave us alone.

Keith: Umm hmm.

B.B.: And it was just like that. I just…I thought I had the right to treat my condition just like the doctor told me to do in California. But as soon as I cross that line into Utah, I lose my rights to self-protection, I lose all my assets, and with the setups that were happening, you see how things were put into place.

Keith: It sounds like you had some friends or at least some acquaintances that ah… didn't much care for you.

B.B.: I could name them; they were with me for years.

Keith: Or, they were trying to further themselves at your expense.

B.B.: Here's the deal, Keith, the worst part of it. I don't care about losing it; I gained it once. I lost 5… you know, I had 5 addresses in Utah when that judge said you've got 48 hours to get out of the state; I had to sell investment properties for a loss, I…I just dumped and left. I was able to keep my truck I had for 26 years; I kept my Jeep I had for over 20 years. But we...I...and the moment I decided the most important thing was to keep my family together. Nothing else mattered; I could lose it all; I made it once; I could make it again; it doesn't matter.

Keith: Sure.

B.B.: But the betrayal of people around me like that, that were, you know...

Keith: Oh sure...

B.B.: You know I lead an exciting life, so somebodies like, where are you going? Are you going to L.A.? Is anybody riding with ya? You're just going to the beach. You got a meeting, okay, I'll...can I go? You know what I mean? I'm like yeah, sure, you can ride. So these people that were free, I'm like yeah, I got a houseboat on Lake Powell, I had four boats, I had five jeeps, I had a race truck, ya know I had the Porsche Cayenne, which that's a whole nother story in itself. And I have an identical car to that right now. I've had it for quite a while; I've only put 1300 miles on it. You've got to have one car that's just the garage queen. So to me, it wasn't weird to have a car for three years, a high-end car that isn't licensed or insured. I had a lot of friends that did that kind of stuff.

Keith: Mmm-hmm.

B.B.: I had a fleet of 12 cars, and I had other people's cars that I stored and maintained too.

Keith: Right, I mean it's.... we just need to clear the air, right?

B.B.: Yeah, definitely and...and... you ..know that's why we should meet, though. Cause there is... it's... it's more of a timeline that I would like to go over with ya.

Keith: Absolutely; I mean, that's one of the biggest things to try to figure out what happened, right? It is...

B.B.: I so, you know more of Steve's time...you know Steven's timeline.

Keith: James and I...

B.B.: Yeah, so when he left...and...cause you gotta consider when Steve disappeared, I...if you look at it in a way...August, I was raided, so I'm facing, you know...potentially losing my family, my freedom; I've already lost my guns, like, you know. All hell is breaking loose. Steven...in a way I had...you know...I can only do so much for myself, but I really felt like...like Steven needed some help, and that was one reason I reached out to his dad. And..I..ar..his mom actually paid me, ya know, like most of the money Steven, that Steven owed. So it was never about the money, ya know, it was about making sure Steven was okay.

Keith: Sure.

B.B.: And that's a big reason for all those calls.

Keith: Do you...did you know at the time, did you know Mitch DeMann?

B.B.: No, well, the only, so there may be a link through rock crawling. Because somebody told me they looked up...his Instagram or something. I have no footprint on mine, so it's not; you're not going to find me out there. But he's out there. And part of his Instagram is rock crawling, remote control rock crawling. So as an event organizer, if somebody wanted to remote control rock crawling, one of our organized U-rock events or the SEMA show, or something like that. They would have been directed to me, and I would have asked, okay, what are you doing, when you are going to do it…so there's…no, I don't know him directly…and… and you know, the DeMann name kinda sounds familiar. I spend about 30 days in Vegas every year between the SEMA show and. I…I built some stuff for BAE systems and WRS, and I flew in and out of Henderson Executive Airport quite a bit. Like the more you know, ah…the pharmacy thing was such a small part of it.

Keith: Mmm hmm.

B.B.: To think that…and for…so the other thing is I worked with a guy… it's a Dr. (name) who owns (co-name).

Keith: Mmm-hmm.

B.B.: He has a supplement company, so to this day, when I grab my overnight bag, which everybody has a shower bag with some Tylenol and some supplements in it.

Keith: Sure.

B.B.: There was never a time where I was casually carrying around pharmaceuticals from that pharmacy, ever. Most of the time, my only responsibility was to go in and reorganize those re-packs. Once in a while, there was a blizzard, or something didn't go out. One night, they called me, and they said, all the old people up in Idaho aren't going to get their meds, and I had a jeep with really good tires on it; it was capable of making up through. They knew that they could call on me if I said I would do it; the job was going to get done once I was committed to it; the thing is, I never let 'em down.

Keith: Umm hmm.

B.B.: So, I...off into the night, take all these meds. Um, as soon as I get to town, I find a police officer who escorts me into the facility because I don't know where I am. I bring the meds in, and all the old people cheer and clap, and I get back into my Jeep and drive home. So once in a while, if there was an emergency delivery, I would make that delivery. But most everything they did was, ya know, done other ways. It was only if somebody messed up or something didn't go out; they knew they could count on me to get it there.

Keith: Sure.

B.B.: But most of what I did was just the re-packs. I'd go in for about 1 hour a week; it was like Thursday morning at 10 AM, I'd show up in Layton, so I'd drive from Orem up to Layton or wherever I was, and I'd go in for 1 hour a week, and they paid me that retainer. So, even after they got an anonymous tip that I was stealing from 'em, they knew that wasn't true. They knew me well enough, but they knew it was someone out to get me.

But they had to answer to a board of directors, and all of a sudden, the board of directors is like, well, there's some suspicion for this guy that we're paying like $500 bucks an hour to, ah yeah, maybe we should end this contract. It's been going on for years now. And they didn't need me. They were only paying it cause they... cause I did so well for 'em in the past. And so retained me for emergencies.

Keith: Correct, umm hmm.

B.B.:

So...yeah... that's such a small part of it, so irrelevant. And..and.. everybody's hung up on it, all these podcasts, I've listened to them all, you know, I've read all the comments. I get information from all over the place. So I've tried to follow it and tried to stay out of it. I really don't think it's beneficial for me to talk about it at all. My sister's an attorney and would freak out. James's talked to her; she's... she's feisty, that's not my mom. Please never contact my mom or dad or any family member.

Keith: We won't contact anybody if we have an open...line...you know what I mean?

B.B.: I appreciate that. Did you recognize this number, by the way?

Keith: No...James is the one...

B.B.: It's the same number I've had for 25 years; it's the same number in all the reports.

Keith: Umm hmm.

B.B.: I was making fun of you guys 'cause I'm like, they can't find me, but I have the same phone number for 25 years?

Keith: The problem is those reports get redacted..so...

B.B.: So what about that redacted number? Why, and what

about the AT&T stuff?

Keith: What do you mean?

B.B.: There's just so many suspicious things about the phone and that redacted number. Did we ever figure that out? Was it some ranch in Idaho or something like that? That number went to the next day.

Keith: So, we'd have to talk to James about what we found on that, umm, I mean, I honestly....

B.B.: So have James bring everything.

Keith: Yeah, I've left most of this up to him, ummm, 'cause he's so close to the family, umm....

B.B.: The other thing is I've had a lot of time to think about this since I was out last December. I've put a lot of thought into this, and a lot of things have come up that could be helpful, and I really think with all the interest in it right now, with the (podcaster) and a (podcaster) like there are enough people out there.

Keith: And really, that was really our whole goal is to get people talking to say, hey, I know something, right?

B.B.: Yeah...yeah. And If I did, like whatever I knew, like, I fully cooperated with the police, ya know, I didn't go in Justin's room cause I didn't know what was up with Justin, all a sudden he's gone, and then Steven's gone too, so you know, I didn't...Steven, er...ah... Steven's door was unlocked, and his family had already got his stuff. But Justin's door, I never went in there until the police actually broke in. And when they went in, it was just emptied out. There was some broken furniture or something, and then you could see on a shelf where they had rolled a blunt, and so there was just some dust, some marijuana dust was there.

Keith: Gotch you.

B.B.: And so I, you know, at the time, you can see why I made it clear, nope, that's not mine (giggles). I don't wanna get in trouble for that too. My stash would have been somewhere else. That's not mine; you know what I mean? I'll own it. Cause I'm fully... I'm an advocate of it.

Keith: Yeah.

B.B.: In fact, here's another thing, in the early days of me meeting with my bishop, and saying yeah, I smoke marijuana, or eat, or use marijuana as a medicinal.

Keith: Umm hmm.

B.B.: And I'm, you know, prescribed by a doctor to do so; he said, well, there are general authorities that take prescriptions, let's write a letter to the first counselor, and...th...th...so my bishop met with the...are you LDS?

Keith: No, James is though.

B.B.: Okay, so it...so he will understand the hierarchy. The bishop meets with the stake president, the stake president came to my house, and he said, you know, the only, so if you're legal and California and hold this advanced...in the priesthood you should be able to do it here. The only difference is it's illegal, and the only thing the church has against the use of marijuana is that it's illegal. And so, If I'm in California, it's not illegal, but if I'm in Utah, it is. So, they wrote a letter to the first president, who wrote a letter back saying, if he has complied with the doctor's orders, if he's prescribed it, then, you know, the only problem is it's illegal, so he's got to go somewhere where it's not. You can't break the law, but there's no problem with it otherwise, especially if it's prescribed.

Keith: Right.

B.B.: And so ever since then, I've done everything I can to comply, even to the point, like I'm not recklessly out sitting out on the porch smoking a doobie, no I'm paying taxes on it, I'm paying the doctor to prescribe it, I get checkups, they...ya know...I don't take any other pharmaceuticals; I haven't since like 2007 probably was the last time I took a pharmaceutical; I don't take aspirin, I don't drink, and I don't cuss. Like me, and Steven got along great. So...the idea out there, that you know, I'm some sort of hardened criminal, I'll admit to my wrongdoings. And I...push limits...or I used to.

Keith: But yeah, that's like one of the things we said; just because there is this in his past does not make him a bad person. It does not make you...

B.B.: You know you called me a clean one owner at one point, I'm driving down the freeway, and my wife and I were just laughing at this, like... it's a... it's a...

Keith: Well, ya know.

B.B.: So...it's... It did get, ya know, it wasn't slander; sometimes it was slander. James said a few things that you corrected. You know, like, there was the probation, compared to parole, prison compared to jail. Like that sentence...after that one case where they said I had to go to jail for ten days, but they gave me credit for three days served, so they said you gotta go to jail for seven days and take a misdemeanor. I'm like, dude, put the misdemeanor on the pile. I'll get some sleep for seven days.

Keith: Right.

B.B.: So I go into...so... I was supposed to check into jail, you have to read the court transcript, but they misread and mistyped, so... they thought I was supposed to be in jail on December 29, well they gave me a month; it wasn't supposed to be until January 29, and the judge acknowledged it, that's why that judged gave me that $300-dollar credit like 60 days later, cause he was like oh whoops sorry. You know, you just spent like 49 days in jail instead of 7

Keith: Wow.

B.B.: Because once...so the... the jailer called me on December 29, and he said, aren't you reporting today, because they had my phone number, I'm like, no, I don't need to report for a month, and the jailer said, well there's nothing I can do about that, I have a court order saying you're supposed to be here, so I have to just put you in contempt of the court order. I called my attorney; he's like, no, I heard it too, the judge knows that don't worry about it, he's like, just let it roll for a month, so I was in the back canyons of Utah for most of that January before I went in and surrendered myself on the day I was supposed to. Well, once you're in jail, it's up to the jail when they release you so that seven days turned into seven weeks before they let me out. Held against my will, with my attorneys...I couldn't get through to my attorneys. I couldn't use the phone; it was like, my wife almost had a nervous breakdown; they put her on Paxil, and it took us six weeks to get her off after I got out. And then, a probation officer showed up at my house unannounced and found one little nug (nugget) of marijuana, and I went back in for 60 days. So that year, 2012, I spent a hundred days in jail. With no...no....no a....no victim cause I had a little bit of marijuana, and when it should have been seven days. I agreed to spend seven days, yeah.

Keith: Wow, that's changed nowadays, huh... as far as...

B.B.: Well yeah, it's not even illegal now, and I knew it wouldn't be. To me... Diet Coke should be illegal.

Keith: Right.

B.B.: To me. I was using, like, a natural source, and ..I... I'm..you know, I eat clean.

Keith: Umm hmm.

B.B.: I still weigh and look the same as I did in High School. I just drove 12 hours from San Francisco; you can tell I'm all wired up, but, yeah, it was like, it was a long night listening to your podcast; I'm like, man, that's it; he flushed me out, like I'm going, I'm gonna call em I... what's your...Exclusive right? Exclusive speculation, no ah, Exclusive accusation, oh no, it's Exclusive investigation right, then I was like no, I don't wanna come up on the rung for it. But then I'm like, he's been insulting me for three podcasts. What am I afraid of, ya know?

Keith: Well, it's certainly....

B.B.: I know…I…I know… but… it's gone around the block now. Every podcast is saying the same stuff, and it's like this circular reading where it's just getting worse. And…and I would love to see the Steven Kocher case solved…

Keith: Don't we all?

B.B.: Bad enough to put myself out there to say start over, clear the drawing board, your way off. And for me, look at it from my point of view. Steven's case is so mysterious, and it doesn't make sense, but it's really easy to just push it off on the landlord and go on to the next case. Right, look at the comment.

Keith: Right, and I honestly don't think it's…

B.B.: And now look at it from my point of view; I know the landlord didn't do it. It is that mysterious.

Keith: Right.

B.B.: What did happen? What really happened? And the other thing is, if I was under federal indictment, Steven lived at my house with me, the stolen car that was part of this high-end theft ring, the big interstate federal deal with witnesses, you know this was a big thing. Steven would have been under; there are three levels of separation, right? If I'm under federal investigation, they can investigate everybody I know, and then they can go a step further into everybody they know, these, you know about this, right?

Keith: Yep

BB: So why...why do we even think Steven wasn't under surveillance at the time, and the reason they really didn't work that hard on the case is because they already know what happened.

Keith: Yeah, maybe, and that's...you know..lets...I mean lets...lets do that I mean...

B.B.: Yeah, and I don't wanna sound like I'm deflecting, but these are things we need to consider. This is a scary situation.

Keith: ...look at it from our point of view too...all we have is paper, right?

B.B.: Yeah.

Keith: We've got court records, we've got some reports that are redacted. Umm, some reports aren't, but most are redacted, umm, so we've got to try to piece it together, and really the only connection that you have is your probably the last person who talked to him.

B.B.: Over the phone, possibly. Yeah, and see, bring whatever you have. Cause those details. I don't remember. But whatever I told the police back then, yeah, I was forthcoming; whatever I had, I wanted them to know 'cause I knew I was under surveillance. And I wasn't a suspect.

Keith: And we don't necessarily think that you are; I mean, we have Steven's phone records, and really, some of the biggest questions are, why were you trying to call him? He was missing, I mean, was..you know, was it some, was it because of his life...you know what I mean?

B.B.: Nope, because he couldn't answer this phone, and I'm like, oh.

Keith: Something's up. Right.

B.B.: Yeah, 'cause he answered my calls before. And I only talked to him once in a while, and he'd have a plan, and his plan was, I'm going to move on, I'm going to do something else, I'm going to pay you when I have the money, and his mom and dad, I talked to them, they were like we have the money, don't worry about it, like, ya know. I…I…took Justin to court; I…wouldn't of with Steve, like I and he had an agreement. Steven didn't sneak out the window in the middle of the night; you know what I mean?

Keith: Right…right.I gotcha.

B.B.: So that should tell ya a lot about Justin, and that whole Hummer story, now… I'm..in Justin's defense, I did have a Hummer, and I did have it at the house in St. George, on my way to go up north and pick up my family, we spent a few days out on the San Rafael Swell, and then I dropped it off back in Vegas when I flew to Texas to do that job at Ft. Bliss. When I got back from Texas, my F250 Diesel was already in Vegas, so I didn't need to rent anything else. But during that time, it..so..for two weeks er so preceding the time I went to Ft. Bliss, I had the Hummer. When I was at Ft. Bliss when that vehicle got rolled, It was a prototype of that vehicle.

Keith: Uh huh.

B.B.: It got flipped end over end with four people in it, a big catastrophe that shut down the operation. That was the one I had pictures of that just mysteriously disappeared. So, you know, I may have mentioned that story to Justin. And he probably just got them mixed up. Cause…I am on a…I was…ya know, during the month of October, two of the weeks, I had a Hummer. It was just as a civilian. It was rented from Enterprise-rent-a-car, and then two of the weeks, I was a civilian contractor working with the SRATS program with the U.S. Army directly, on base, with full clearance and background checks; you can imagine what I went through to work for BAE systems…

Keith: Oh yeah.

B.B.: And the U.S. Army and the SRATS program and Lucas Oil. I mean, Miller MotorSports Park, these were big names. My resume gets me hired. Like a lot of these places, any of the legitimate places, ah…a couple of em I had to respectfully resign from over anonymous emails that they would get, things like that. I was like, look, ya know. They're like. We don't believe it; everything is cool. We'll give you a great final recommendation for whatever you wanna do. If anybody calls us, we love you. But it's like yeah, I'll just respectfully resign. I've got plenty of other things to do. Most of what I do is, like, short term anyway, ya know, it's a show or event where the show must go on. Ya know, so I get…I get things done. But it's just; it's my specialty.

Keith: Look, I mean, you actually sound like a pretty cool dude. Um, let's clear the air, let's put it out there, then we can do it. I'll bring you on; we can do…

B.B.: Ahh…Im… I'm not looking for that, though. That's why

I wanna talk to you before you put anything out; I said the same thing to (podcaster) I...I called him up, and I was like, look, here are a few things; I sent him a bunch of Youtube clips, I said, you just need to watch these, this is what I was really into, and I sent him some of the Youtube stuff of the offroad racing, and you can find the SRATS on Youtube, you can see the vehicles. So I sent him some of that, and I was like, you know, this...look at the bigger picture, this is the stuff that's out there that's public. I'm not disclosing anything I shouldn't be, you know.

Keith: Sure.

B.B.: Normally, I don't consent to searches, and I don't answer questions. That's all you need to know about me; I don't answer questions. Why not? You just asked me a question (giggles). I don't answer questions.

Keith: I get that.

B.B.: That's it. It's my 5th Amendment right not to incriminate myself. And I wish I would have known now what I knew then; I would have never gotten into any of that trouble. So much of the trouble I got in was like me being like, oh, I didn't answer their questions.

Keith: Yeah.

B.B.: Yeah, and luckily, I survived, and I'm still breathing free air. But, ya know, my wife is really concerned about this blowback on my kids, all this podcast stuff; there are people in the comments that are looking for me. There are people that think they've figured out where I am now.

Keith: Well, let's clear that and...

B.B.: Well, I'll be up that way...I could be there, like Utah County on Friday.

Keith: Um, I mean, I think Friday will work. I just need to call James. I've got...

B.B.: You guys out of Salt Lake County or further north?

Keith: Salt Lake, but we're on the south end.

B.B.: If I had to, I could meet you up there, but.

Keith: Well, we could meet you wherever, coffee shop, thanksgiving point. I don't care; you know what I mean.

B.B.: Yeah, that be cool, something like that. Yeah, I really wanna meet you guys since you were hired by the family. I got nothing really to say to anybody else. The family I care about. When I found out about (Steven's father's name), yeah, that's, but yeah, I can see, I'm probably not the first to call you out on speculation and the accusations that I heard by your third, you started talking about, you know, making corrections.

Keith: Yeah, I mean, you're the first person that's actually called based on the podcasts; I mean, we are talking to DeMann now, um, as a result of just persistence, not the podcast really.

B.B.: I would love to know if there is a link.

Keith: Right. And that's what we really want too...

B.B.: See you; the other thing is the hard drive. The answer's gotta be on the hard drive.

Keith: Well, I have it; in fact, I have the whole fucking machine; oops, sorry.

B.B.: How do we get into it? What can you crowdsource that can you put? Alright, we gotta talk. This is big

Keith: I mean, look, we're not here to make anybody look bad…

B.B.: No, and I don't care if I do look bad. When you look at my reputation…you know how many convictions I have compared to how many charges.

Keith: Right…but on paper, you look not so great, right? It's like…

B.B.: I don't need to look good; I ain't looking for a job.

Keith: It doesn't matter…

B.B.: No, it doesn't…

Keith: It's about what happened and…

B.B.: So here, Keith, here's part of the reason all that happened is because, like, even in this way I live now. Like, I don't work for anybody here, I work for other people outside of town, so nobody has any control…like people see me in the store whatever, like, ya know, I have to kind of, with everything that's happened to me in the past and the level of betrayal and sabotage.

Keith: Sure.

B.B.: You can see why I have never posted anything online ever, anywhere. Not on Facebook, nothing, ever, and..so you know this goes way back, this isn't just a recent...this has been going on with me since...

Keith: No. there are people back.....two thousand...

B.B.: But this goes on the way before Steven.

Keith: Right, right.

B.B.: I've had that car three years before, Steven. I...I...got it; it was like September 2005 or anyway, yeah.

Keith: Like I said...like I said, on paper, if you look at you on paper, It's like, where are all these unanswered questions....

B.B.: Well, and that's the thing, too; I can add more to that paper that makes it look worse, like flying in and out of Henderson Executive Airport. And that I had a Scottsdale address for a while. It's like, this is all perfectly explainable, but it looks...but it looks....and none of that hit the internet, though ...

Keith: (unintelligible) right?

B.B.: No, but none of that hit the internet, though, like the more that comes out, the worse I'm gonna look until we get going in the right direction.

Keith: Well...well then, let's do it. I mean, so what's your availability Friday? Could you do that in the morning, like 10 o'clock?

B.B.: That probably would work best, yeah.

Keith: So...let me get with...with ah James, and then is this the cell phone I can text you on?

B.B.: Yeah.

Keith: K, I'll text you a confirmation, I'll get you an address to a coffee shop or something up there, and like Thanksgiving point....

B.B.: And I also understand also about, you know, something, your podcast and putting your information out, and freedom of speech, you can say whatever you want about this conversation, I...I..understand that, but I would ask like...

Keith: We're not gonna...(unintelligible.)

B.B.: Maybe get on the same page first.

Keith: Ah..ah..ah.. I really, that's what I would prefer....

B.B.: Then maybe even a, ya know, whatever you wanna release to some other people to get crowdsourcing going, there are some podcasts that, ya know, before we just bash em, let's use em.

Keith: Yeah. And let's talk about that for... maybe we could...

B.B.: Yeah, absolutely.

Keith: Umm, I mean, we don't have a.. umm, a...a...umm recording scheduled. There are a couple more episodes that are going to come out, umm, one will probably be released this week, um, but it takes us up to, ya know, a jacket that we found, umm...

B.B.: Yeah, with the DNA on the jacket, so I bet that DNA comes back to a guy name S.W., and I don't know if that's his real name, but I would have had a lot of army jackets and a lot of military gear like that, and it would be, it's not a surprise that I would have hid a pipe with cops searching my garage all the time, yeah I would have stuck a coat up in the top of the garage with a pipe or something in it, ya know. That's not shocking, but my personnel assistant S.W., was ah...often borrowed clothes of mine and ended up bleeding a lot; he wasn't the smartest guy, had a bald head, and bumped his head a lot; there's a good chance it will come back to him. You could find out what his real name is, but he's all over the discovery. In September 2009, he was the one that made th, the reason they were able to get a warrant. But then I had them under surveillance, when they had me under surveillance, and I was able to beat their surveillance, and the warrant expired. That was during the time of the shutdown when the government shutdown happened; I was out on my houseboat at Lake Powell, and Lake Powell shut down. Yeah, so there's a lot to it.

Keith: Okay...well...let me...let me get with James; he can check his availability for Friday...

B.B.: Did you get the information then? Thats...thats.

Keith: We have...well...so there are a couple of different tests, we do have DNA on the jacket ah....

B.B.: And so you can match it with Koecher...

Keith: Well... it's been confirmed that it's male DNA.

B.B.: Okay.

Keith: There's another test that potentially has to be done to get even one step further, which would potentially be an identity, umm,...

B.B.: so... okay...if you can bring me, or text me a picture of that coat, I might have a better explanation of it, cause it could have come from...

Keith: James will have a picture of it...

B.B.: Yeah, it could have come from a second-hand store; it could have come from, like, one of the jobs I did, ya know.

Keith: The patches were removed, but it was probably; I think, there was a rank to it that you could see like the outline of where the patches were...

B.B.: But see, that was the kind of stuff, I had a lot of that around, and, that dude S was with me, S.W. was with me for like three plus years, he was the one that lived right around the corner, confidential informant, like, he came down to Arizona one day, and I showed him in the discovery, I said, this is you, you were the only one in my garage that whole month of September. You were the confidential informant, the buyer, or whatever they called it. And he admitted to it, he said, maybe they unwittingly used me. And I was like, just own it, just tell me what happened, you know.

Keith: Umm hmm.

B.B.: And he wouldn't. He said they unwittingly used me, so I said, get in the truck, and I drove him to the bus stop down in Phoenix. I gave him enough money for a Greyhound ticket, and I never saw him again.

Keith: Wow.

B.B.: Yeah, but he was one of my...like a best friend, like a travel companion, as you know, he was obviously, obviously working with the major crimes task force, for sure, for years. He was the problem. He kept trying to get me to build fully automatic guns, and I wouldn't do it. I had no reason to, I...you know... it's ridiculous, especially after the trouble I'd seen, know what I mean...so.

Keith: Right. Alright, B, let me get a hold of James, and let's plan on Friday at 10...

B.B.: The latest is the better cause I'll be, I'll likely be...yeah, let me know what he thinks, and then I'll confirm from there.

Keith: Okay, yeah, we can...

B.B.: I'll be in a rental car; it might be a different one than you see next time.

Keith: Okay (giggles)

B.B.: (giggles) alright, I look forward to meeting you.

Keith: Okay, bye.

Call ends.

After reading all of that, and in my case, hearing all of that, one does necessarily have to admit it. Mr. B. is quite an alluring and maybe even pivotal character in the Koecher case, isn't he? He's charismatic, alright. Likes to talk about his life, obviously. And appears successful to some extent. From a government contractor with (BAE) testing military vehicles in the (SRATS program,) his participation in SEMA shows and his affiliation as a shadow member of the L.D.S. church. Let's not forget how he describes himself as a dependable "old peoples" medication delivery person as well. Mr. B. gladly shares his life experiences, both good and bad. He describes the mysterious removal of pictures from his phone, the raids on his house, bobbing in Lake Powell on his houseboat, and mistakenly spending 100 days in jail.

I couldn't help but smell an odor of criminality, not just because of all the criminal behavior he participated in, but also as B.B. spoke of his past. Saying, "I can add more to that paper that makes it look worse, like flying in and out of Henderson Executive Airport. Or "...like the more that comes out, the worse I'm gonna look..." I got an impression, as he spoke, that he is almost claiming to be a victim of circumstances and the police somehow. Did you get that sense too?

It would also be very interesting to know more about the so-called anonymous emails to employers that B.B. worked for. One of which resulted in his dismissal after he was accused of stealing medications. And, according to B.B. himself, there were other anonymous emails resulting in further dismissals from employers. What was going on there? What was B.B. up to?

Did you pick up on the possible, not-so-subtle, not-so-circumstantial connection between M.D. and B.B.? In discussing the radio-controlled rock crawler events, which B.B. organized. He made it sound like participants were required to go through him in order to engage in an event. B.B. talks of M.D.'s Instagram account having references to this hobby. How does B.B. know that?

When Keith asks B.B. straight out if he knew M.D. He says not personally, but does recognize the DeMann name. He even hints at the possibility of being connected to M.D. through the rock crawler events somehow. This is a clue. A possible connection between the two persons is vitally important here.

The Suspicious Property

Remember the damage in the Casita, which M.D. took ownership of causing in the previous interviews? Well, I believe the possibility certainly does exist that Steven could be buried on that home's property, where M.D. lived for a time. James located and reached out to the property owner in an attempt to receive permission to search and perhaps run a cadaver dog over that property. I also believe this home should be eliminated as a possible final resting place for Steven Koecher. The owner declined the request to search. Here is the email from the owner in response to James' request:

July 26, 2020

"Hello James,

Thank you for your email and for bringing me up to date on your case.

I've spoken with my attorney regarding your request to run the cadaver dogs on my property. However, upon his advice, I am declining your request. I have not been presented with any compelling evidence that warrants this search. Rather, it's more your desire to eliminate an obscure possibility to solve a 10-year-old case. While I respect your desire, I cannot assist you at this time.

My attorney correctly points out that the negative potential financial impact on my property's value would be substantial in the unlikely event that the dogs were to indicate that further excavation would be necessary. Moreover, if excavation were to become necessary, I cannot rely solely on your well-meaning assurances that I would suffer no adverse impact. You'll no doubt agree that I've been cooperative with you thus far, on several occasions providing backstory, pictures of the Casita, contact information for (redacted,) (redacted) and (redacted.) However, I must decline your present request.

Later this week, I'm headed to Washington until late September. My attorney has outlined a possible solution to your issue, which we can discuss once I return."

Kind Regards,

JB

To my knowledge, several subsequent attempts to communicate again with this homeowner went un-responded to.. The only way to search the property now is via a police search warrant, unless the owner sells and a new owner takes possession of the home who might then provide permission.

What the homeowner might want to consider is, eliminating his property as a possible burial ground. It could curtail any doubt which may currently surround this property and may already impede the home's value. It's very likely people have read or heard about the case and know of the address in question.

If there is even the slightest possibility Steven is buried

there, you, sir, have a duty to the family of the murdered son, to the siblings, and to his deceased father. You see sir, that address has been publicized in so many different podcasts and in many different internet stories over the years. Written down in a record of digital history. To the owner, I ask, "Help us eliminate that property, please."

In my view, there is enough evidence now to execute a search warrant on that property i,e, The video, Steven's last seen proximity so close to the home, the formerly unknown neighbor interacting with Steven, the comments from the neighbor who lived across the street from the DeManns and the detective who states he saw activity at that house when he was there, not to mention his gut feeling after interviewing M.D.

A Former MD Girlfriend and A Bomber Jacket

As I have said here before, I must say again, James has done an excellent job of finding people, and evidence connected to this case. In a police record regarding M.D. and his propensity for domestic violence involving his former girlfriends, James Baker managed to find one former girlfriend of M.D. 's in October 2022. I'm going to identify her only as Franny here. Franny would only text with J.B. for unknown reasons. He made a valiant effort to get her to speak on the phone, but she declined. Here is a text thread between him and Franny:

"Y can't we just text?" she asks. James asks Franny about her relationship with M.D. "What would you like to ask me or tell me? I'm interested in DeMann," she texts. "Do u just want your question on record? Y do you need to find him? Is he still a criminal? Were u his friend?" She peppers. He explains he's investigating a missing person. "He walked toward M.D.'s home when he disappeared.

We need to talk. I have worked on this for two years. It's hard to explain it all in texts," he says in a text. Franny responds with, "I read a page regarding his disappearance on Websleuths. The DeMann family was always moving after claiming bankruptcy, and Mitch was always nervous…"

"I just listened to a website about Steven's disappearance with regards to Mitch. It all rings true. I have known Mitch for several years, and this is exactly what I know about him and his family's type of behavior. His family was always moving, and Mitch could never get away from them because he was incapable of taking care of himself because he was a drug addict, which is why he said he was afraid of letting anyone know where he lived. Because of people being in their drug lifestyle…"

She continues, "Oh yeah, and after he stole money from me, I pursued him until he filed for a restraining order against me…" In another text, Franny types, "Yes, it's all true. He ruined my life for 5 years. He's an addict narcissist. Everything that (podcaster's name) says about him is consistent with everything I knew about him and his family when they lived in Naples. Every single thing. It is like reliving history listening to this documentary. If his parents put four properties in his name, it's because they had already declared bankruptcy three times and could no longer declare any more." Franny then goes silent. James attempts to reconnect with Franny but with no positive results.

Another intriguing find of J.B.'s that requires mentioning is that of a bomber jacket that was found in the garage ceiling of BB's former residence in Orem.

According to the current owner, who now uses the same garage as an office to conduct his property management business, tells J.B. he found the jacket some time ago. The jacket had some kind of glass pipe in a pocket when he first found it. He disposed of the glass pipe years ago. In addition to the pipe in the pocket, there was also a brown stain of an unknown substance on the back of the jacket near the collar.

The property owner kindly gave J.B. the Jacket, who then took the jacket to Intermountain Forensic, who conducted a field test on the stain. The initial field test produced negative results. J.B. decided to leave the jacket with Intermountain Forensics so they could conduct more extensive testing on it. Further testing on the jacket spot resulted in identifying it as a "human fluid," but due to the degradation of the sample, there was not enough to provide a full profile.

The Lingering Questions

Springtime has got to be my favorite time of the year. The days begin to get longer, and the temperature climbs up, providing a more comfortable time for outdoor activities. In the spring of 2022, I turned some of my attention to preventative maintenance on my home and started different types of landscaping projects surrounding it. During these times of building, digging, painting, or whatever project I was working on, I couldn't help but think about the Koecher case. What the hell happened to Steven?

Going over in my head the storyline, the timeline of events, the persons of interest, the evidence, and how this case has stalled. The one question that kept coming up for me is how we get this story back into the public domain. In addition to asking the question, what is it going to take to get law enforcement to reopen this case? Maybe they won't reopen this case, ever.

The experiences in working with the Henderson police were frustrating. It began to feel as if a stone wall had been constructed, and no one had permission to enter. No further developments, ya know, according to police. However, in a surprise development, in September 2020, James had emailed me regarding a communication he had with his point of contact within the Henderson Police. It was a promising development in the case. Here's the email:

"I was just informed that the POC (point of contact) at HPD has given our information to the Cold Case Unit to review our findings.

He just wanted me to be aware I may get an email from one of them with questions etc.

Hoping this is the start of a good thing!"

J.

My reaction to this email was one of, not only did it sound like a good thing, but quite possibly a reopening of the case, right? I was definitely excited about this new development; of course I was. "The Cold Case Unit was going to look at the case!" Yeah! Well, to my dismay, as of this writing, nothing has ever materialized from HPD's Cold Case Unit that I'm aware of. Ahh damn! Through this tribulation, I found myself wondering if I needed to consider the possibility(s) of the case not only ever getting reopened but rather that it may continue to go unsolved and staying on ice in the cold case units' cold, dark locker. Those two prospects seemed unacceptable to me then, and they still do now.

The subject of missing persons has fascinated me since being introduced to the Steven Koecher case. How does a person just up and vanish? I wanted to do some research on the internet regarding the subject of missing persons. I accidentally came across an author whose subject matter centered around missing persons. And for years now, I have been an avid follower of a world-renowned published author by the name of Dave Paulides.

Mr. Paulides is the creator of the "Canam Missing Project." Canam is short for Canada and America. He has written upwards of 12 books from his "Missing 411" collection. He has produced at least three movies on missing persons in Canada and America. Many of his stories surround missing persons that have occurred in national parks, state parks, wilderness areas, as well as Colleges and Universities in North America and the world.

The missing persons cases he has written about are quite unique from the Koecher case. I believe Koecher met with foul play.

The missing persons cases Dave investigates oftentimes show no evidence of foul play. No evidence surrounding the cause of death either, other than exposure and hypothermia *after* the body is found in freezing temperatures. All you are left with is a mystery. A mystery because many of his missing persons cases cannot be logically explained. Mr. Paulides has been a guest on radio and TV, specifically Coast to Coast AM radio, many times with hosts of the likes of Art Bell, George Noory, and George Knapp. Dave Paulides is a retired law enforcement officer of 25 years, from patrol to serving on a SWAT team, becoming a detective, and serving as part of a Vice/Intelligence Unit, performing various assignments. If you like mysterious disappearances, you'll enjoy reading his books. You'll scratch your head, as I have done after reading about the many cases he's looked at.

Now after having said all that, I was listening to David on his YouTube channel one Sunday morning, as I regularly do, when Dave mentioned George Knapp. Now, If you're familiar with George Knapp, his reputation, his history, and all his work, I need to say no more. If not, you may want to Google George Knapp to learn more about him. George Knapp is part of just a handful of people, if not *the* person, who began to report on and tenaciously investigate the UFO phenomena. George played an instrumental role in bringing the UFO, also known as the UAP phenomenon, out of urban legend and into the contemporary mainstream. George Knapp is quite familiar with the goings on at Skinwalker Ranch in Utah too.

Anyway, Lucky for me, as it turns out, George Knapp is also an investigative journalist in Las Vegas, NV. at KLAS, 8 News now, Las Vegas. The place where George actually reported on hundreds of stories. So, I wondered if He might be willing and interested in helping with this case; I figured nothing ventured, nothing gained, so in June 2022, I sent Mr. Knapp this email:

"Dear Mr. Knapp,

According to Occam's Razor theory, a principle of theory construction or evaluation according to which, other things equal, explanations that posit fewer entities, or fewer kinds of entities, are to be preferred to explanations that posit more. In other words, all things considered, the simplest explanation is probably the correct explanation.

Regarding Steven Koecher's case. He was last seen by at least two witnesses on that fateful day, December 13, 2009. New information has been made public suggesting SK approached a neighbor on Savannah Springs Ave. It should be noted this home is the second house from the end of Savannah Springs. New information suggests this neighbor was interviewed by at least two investigators where he states SK asked him something to the effect of, "Do you want the money?"

The second witness is the video, which captured SK walking by and turning onto Evening Lights. SK first going to the wrong home explains the 6 min gap from arrival to being seen on video. Now, interestingly enough, this witness lived in the second house from the corner of Savannah Springs. A neighbor in the neighborhood across the street from home, located second from the end of Evening Lights, was interviewed, where she stated she saw a moving van, and the people seemed to be moving out quickly that Sunday. This case starts and ends here. It's simple. This is where one person and one surveillance system last saw SK.

In addition, newly uncovered public information reveals the Casita in which M.D. lived was trashed inside by M.D. himself. M.D. had lived there, convalescing from a bad car accident and on many medications. The police finally interviewed M.D. in February 2010, I believe. The police report states his reaction to questioning appeared 'deceptive.' M.D. has a considerable record of domestic violence and drugs. Red Flag!

In my view, the simple explanation is this. S.K. was sent there by someone, whom? I don't know. S.K. visited the wrong house, second from the end of Savanna Springs. Getting his bearings, he begins walking to (redacted) Evening Lights, where he runs into M.D. M.D., high on drugs and out of his mind, having heard "money," beats or strangles S.K. to death. S.K.'s cell is then documented to travel north until it dies. But more importantly, however, investigate the property of (redacted) Evening Lights with a dog and GPR (ground penetrating radar).

The only way to investigate that property is through a warrant. This leads me to my thoughts. A good investigative journalist like yourself could get this back into the public domain. Tell the story of how law enforcement could have done a better job at the time. Give LE another opportunity to investigate; using the new evidence which has been uncovered.

There is ample evidence for another investigation here, in

my opinion. Thirteen years have passed. The public pot will be stirred, perhaps generating tips from current and former co-workers, friends, perhaps a family member of M.D., or even criminals hearing something and wanting to bargain with what they know.

A few days later, to my pleasant surprise, an email appeared in my inbox. An email from George Knapp. "George Knapp responded!! Omg!" I said to myself. Here is his email:

"I am forwarding your note to my I-Team colleagues. These days I am a part-time reporter, working almost entirely from home, and am not able to take on additional projects right now.

Regards,

GK"

Wow! How cool is that? George Knapp has taken an interest in this case and is forwarding my note to his team! How cool is that?? In July 2022. I patiently waited for further contact with all the eagerness of a child on Christmas Eve looking for Santa Clause.

In keeping this squeaky wheel lubricated, I followed up with other emails, and in August 2022, I received an email from one of Mr. Knapp's investigative team members. Mr. David Charns of KLAS, 8 News Now, Las Vegas, was interested in knowing more. He asked what kind of documentation we had and what we believed he could get from the Henderson Police. I told him we had the St. George and Henderson police reports. Mr. Charns and I exchanged a couple of emails and then ultimately spoke on the phone. He agreed to look into broadcasting a story about the case. We had a new development in the case, that of a neighbor who spoke with Steven prior to Steven walking into oblivion.

Near the same time as reaching out to George Knapp in Las Vegas, I also reached out to a KSL television investigative journalist in Salt Lake City. A producer, no less, who I called and, to my amazement, answered the phone! When I explained the reason for my call and relayed how interested I was in having a Steven Koecher piece produced, she recalled how she was somewhat familiar with the story of Steven. Upon conclusion of our conversation, a meeting was scheduled to meet with all of us in Bountiful of all places. The home city of Stevens's parents. I dutifully notified my colleagues, informing them of the interest I had stirred up regarding these conversations I had with KLAS and KSL TV. The producer with KSL agreed to meet all four of us in a park on the west side of Bountiful. As we sat in a park bowery in Bountiful, the elements of the case findings were reviewed and talked about. The meeting concluded with the producer appearing to be interested in doing some story. Since then, I have followed up with this producer via text a few times only to find any story getting broadcasted to be fruitless so far. I am hopeful she will reconnect with us someday because this is as much, if not more, of a Utah story than a Vegas one.

Chapter 22:
Las Vegas Bound

Okay, one down, one to go. We had an investigative journalist in Las Vegas interested in doing a story about Steven. That was something, anyway. Arrangements to meet David in Las Vegas became cemented in a date and time to meet at the studio there in Las Vegas. On the road, I went with Keith driving us down to Las Vegas, James and his wife would be arriving later that day. I was grateful the weather cooperated. I did not want to be driving through Beaver, Utah, in a storm. When traveling, I'm weather conscious and glad when it's over. We had a good time too. On November 14, 2022, at 10AM, we met at the KLAS 8 News Now studio, where we met David and his cameraman Matt. We were well received, introductions were made, and we all moved to a set where the three of us sat. The interview ran approximately 1 hour. After this interview, we all decided to drive down to Henderson and visit the exact location where Steven is recorded driving and walking with purpose before disappearing out of sight.

    I had only viewed the location from a Google Earth perspective, but being there is, of course, totally different. Seeing the home whose cameras recorded the event, seeing the neighbor's home that Steven first approached, and seeing the suspicious home with the Casita in front of it. As I walked around like some tourist taking in the spectacular view, I played that December day in my mind's eye and wondered why Steven came here. Who sent him here, if anyone? I knew exactly where Steven parked his car; I stood there, I walked the same path Steven walked in the video, and I crossed Evening Lights the same as Steven did in the video.

He was only feet from the suspicious house when he walked out of the camera's frame. While there, we learned from the current occupant of the home with the cameras on it that the retired air marshal who owned the home had passed on. Rest in Peace, Sir.

In addition to the television interview, James had made prior arrangements to meet with the neighbor later that day, who had stated Steven knocked on his door the day he vanished. James had spoken in person with this man some time ago, on his way back to Salt Lake after a short Vegas get-a-way. His plan included a request for a Henderson police officer to meet us at the neighbor's house in order to get an official statement from him for the record. This new development would become part of the original case file, and it was hoped it would spur police into investigating the case further.

When Henderson police officer "G" arrived, he was a bit confused as to why he was there but was soon eager to help after a proper briefing to him why. We all walked over to this neighbor's house like so many Men in Black. The neighbor's door was knocked on, and he opened it to see the three of us, along with a uniformed Henderson police officer standing on his stoop. We were invited in. It became apparent to me that the Mrs. was none too happy we were there, justifiably so I suppose. Strangers in her home, along with a uniformed police officer, would make many people uncomfortable. And some folks just do not want to be involved. I get it.

However, some people can feel it's incumbent on them to do the right thing too. I had a sense this man felt compelled to report what he experienced that day in December 2009, ergo, do the right thing. Nonetheless, he requested he not be identified if KLAS 8 News now wanted an interview. I understand that request too. Both of these fine people might believe whoever is responsible for Steven's disappearance, may want them to keep quiet.

Once we were all in a room in the home, officer "G" began asking routine questions, such as his name of this neighbor as it's spelled on his driver's license. After the routine questions concluded, the neighbor began reporting how he was home that day using the restroom. He either heard a knock on the door or the doorbell. After gathering himself together and eventually getting to the door, he opened it to see Steven on the walk in front of the home. It was here when Steven said something about money. Do you have the money? Do you need the money? Something along those lines.

After the neighbor presumably reacts to this strange question, whether he said I don't know what you're talking about or says no, Steven walks away and begins walking east toward Evening Lights. This is the 6-minute gap explained, from the time when Steven was recorded arriving in his car to being recorded walking in the video. Steven approaches the wrong house first.

This witness is indeed providing more evidence, and it clearly is a new development in the case. This would make the neighbor the first to see Steven in the area. The video is the second witness to record Steven. For all intents and purposes, this neighbor is most likely the last person to speak with Steven before he disappears.

Either way, Steven is witnessed and recorded as being in the area that day and at that time. He walks north on Evening lights and out of view. I want to thank Officer G for his professional conduct and the impeccable demeanor he showed in assisting us that night. Thank you, sir!

The Broadcast

On November 21, 2022, KLAS, 8 News Now, Las Vegas, broadcasted our interview to their evening audience. The story first began by highlighting the infamous video of Steven's arrival again, as many have done prior. A Deja Vu moment, as it were.

Haven't we been here before? That video has always been an opener for a Steven Koecher story. After all, it had already been part of other broadcasts and podcasts numerous times.

Mr. Charns provided the narration along with our

comments about the case, as is a practice for news organizations to do. All were spliced together and then made into the story they ran. What was a 1-hour interview became an edited 5 minutes of news. Not to sound begrudging, it still pleased me some because Steven Koecher's name and some of the circumstances surrounding his disappearance were broadcast to the world again. So much information about this case is circulating, and 5 minutes of news seems like an injustice. I understand though, time is money. Other informative news stories need to be broadcast.

There is much news out there needing attention. I get it. We were not allowed to mention any names of actual persons of interest on camera or the suspicious address on Evening Lights. Too many lawyers are standing by to bring an action, I presume. Ironically, the names of those persons and the suspicious property address, all have been verbalized in many podcasts since Steven's disappearance. In writing this, I have chosen not to use any real names of persons of interest, the suspicious address, investigators involved, or the agency involved, for different reasons. However, the initials used are the actual initials.

Notwithstanding, anyone who is familiar with this case or has heard any podcasts about it, may very well have already heard and will hear if listened to, the real names of persons involved in this case. Those persons interviewed by investigators, M.D. and B.B. in particular, openly admit to listening to different podcasts.

As the days ticked by after the broadcast, I began wondering if I should begin accepting the fact that this broadcast, however, intended, turned into just another contemporary story about Steven Koecher, "the missing person," compared to Steven Kocher the person, the man, the brother, the son, who's still missing, and who did not abandon his car. Don't get me wrong; I graciously accepted the help in keeping the case alive and trying to prevent it from refreezing.

I convey my sincere gratitude to Mr. Knapp and Mr. Charns for their efforts. To my pleasant surprise, a second story ran on KLAS days later regarding the neighbor who spoke to Steven about money on the day he went missing. I was not expecting a follow-up story. This should have been considered as new evidence and should have been written into the case file by the Henderson police officer who heard it..

The neighbor had been contacted, approached, and interviewed. Very cool! He tells his story of what he experienced that day. He was not identified at his request, I figured he wouldn't be. Can't blame the guy. If it were me, it wouldn't be the fear of retaliation for knowing who I was, so much as the desire to be anonymous. I like my anonymity. I was happy to hear it broadcast into cyberspace and to the world again. A new development, if you will, was finally broadcast. This neighbor was missed somehow by police in December 2009. This is, at minimum, one new development; in truth, more like real evidence. Eyewitness testimony.

A No-Body Homicide

When a person goes missing, police are reluctant to say a crime has occurred for a variety of reasons. They either turn up alive, or they are found dead. Either way they are found.

This could be why police tend to wait and see.

In Steven's case, he was having some financial difficulties, that's a given. It appears his life was moving along like many of ours do. Sure, there are ups and downs in our lives. But not to the point of suicide, right?. A permanent solution to a temporary situation is a bad choice. Therefore, I believe Steven committing suicide can be ruled out, really. The evidence suggests he intended on returning to his car and spending the holiday with his family.

In addition, he has not turned up anywhere since disappearing, alive or dead. So, I believe we can rule out that he disappeared himself too. Both possible manners are incongruent with the facts of this case. Steven had every intention of returning to his car that day. Steven or his body has eluded discovery so far.

No examination of his body has been made to determine a cause or manner of death. By this time, it may be difficult to determine a manner of death if his remains are ever found. But we all know his remains are somewhere, don't we? All the police had to go on at the time was a so-called abandoned vehicle. In actuality, it was an empty vehicle. Abandon suggests he would not be returning to it. Of course he had intended to return to it. There were Christmas presents in it, purchased the day before, when it was found.

Due to the many, many missing persons reports assigned to police every year, and as many of those take care of themselves, whether the person returns, or is found dead somewhere, police tend to "wait and see" or prioritize the case as just a missing person rather than a crime and "wait and see" some more. I believe this happened here.

This flawed practice causes a case to easily lose momentum and become just part of the workload along with the other missing-person cases. Often, police do not capture timely eyewitnesses or interviews; it's just a missing person case, after all. A likely scenario is this case was delayed for two weeks due to the approaching holiday.

Consequently, timelines can blur, and memories can fade. However, when facts and circumstances indicate a strong possibility of foul play, police should consider the missing person case as a potential homicide. I believe Steven Koecher met with foul play and was murdered that day. Subsequently, we can presume his body was secretly disposed of somewhere. Having said that, again it follows that his body's remains are somewhere aren't they? The body itself provides the best evidence of an unlawful death.

This is why I am adamant about searching the suspicious property with a dog on Evening Lights, as well as the new property Sam DeMann moved into, which lies only 1-mile southwest of the Evening Lights address. I'd run a dog through two more places: The U-haul self-storage center near the I515/Russel road interchange and the Extra Space Storage, both are very close to Evening Lights and each other..

Running a dog through these places may not result in finding remains initially, but a dog can pick up the smell of human decay, even after the body has been moved. I've seen it done; when one dog I've watched located a burial location, after the body had been moved. The noses on those types of dogs are phenomenal. The science behind scent is rather precise. Decomposition odor sticks to things and lingers for a long time.

Remember in the Tarot card reading how we were told Steven would likely be found by accident? Those properties should be eliminated as possible holding areas and the two residences as possible burial sites.

Other ways exist to determine that a person died. Homicide investigators have been known to base their cases on circumstantial evidence. 1) that the victim is dead; 2) that the person had been murdered; 3) the approximate time; 4) that the likely location of the crime is within their jurisdiction and 5) a potential suspect.

As in many homicides, perpetrators and victims often know each other, and the perpetrators, more often than not, have a motive to commit a homicide. A motive in this case could be money, especially after money was talked about with the neighbor. I don't believe B.B. actually committed murder, but even his story includes back rent.

Let us apply these 5 noted pieces of circumstantial evidence to the Koecher case.

1) I believe Steven Koecher is dead; most people believe that, too; 2) That he was murdered. He or his body has not been located after 13 plus years due to the body presumably being concealed; 3) Time of death. December 13, 2009, around noon. Remember we have evidence (video and testimony to police) of his last known location there. 4) The likely location of his

homicide is Henderson, NV., and 5)

I believe there is one solid person of interest in this case. I'll go as far as calling him a suspect in the murder of Steven Koecher. And I would identify one other person of interest who could be considered complicit. Not in the act of murder itself, but rather in knowing something crucial. If that person would just come forward, perhaps he could bargain with this knowledge. He could request or be granted immunity perhaps. After all, if he did not commit the murder and his information could lead police to the killer, then why not explore that option?

I also believe the killer did not commit a pre-planned, intentional murder, but rather seized on a delusional opportunity where events unfolded out of control which then resulted in Steven's death. When police talk of a motive, means, and opportunity in a crime, they are attempting to pin down potential suspects. The motive, in this case, would be money wouldn't it? The means would be someone over 6 feet tall and 200 pounds. They could easily overcome someone like Steven, who is reported to be 5 feet 11 inches tall and 180 pounds; add a weapon in the mix, a knife, a hammer, or a baseball bat, and Steven would not stand a chance. The opportunity existed when the killer and Steven were alone together. Perhaps Steven resisted and fought back. I have no idea. I hope he did.

In Conclusion

I hope I have done at least a satisfactory job in outlining the facts of this case up to now and in presenting them to the reader. The aggregate of the facts in this story needed to be assembled and written down, making it a first of its kind. Steven could still be considered just a missing person, I suppose. However, this missing person affected many, many people. The effects of him going missing still reverberate in the minds and hearts of those many to this day.

In Chicago, Illinois, the Chicago police department has established a missing person unit dedicated to finding missing persons. It is my understanding when a person is reported missing, someone in the unit is assigned to begin an investigation into their whereabouts forthwith. How fortunate it would have been to have had something like that when Steven disappeared.

I do consider myself an advocate of the police, not a cop-wanna-be. No, but rather a supportive concerned citizen. The police have so much on their plate these days, and it's no wonder many are leaving, some even committing suicide. How sad is that? Without law enforcement, a society can devolve into chaos pretty quickly. Nearly all of us delegate our own responsibility of protection and the protection of those we love to the police. "I can't or won't protect myself in hopes the police will" is really the rationale, isn't it? Police cannot be in all places at all times, either. Always remember, when seconds count police are just minutes away.

The concerned citizen is a law-abiding, tax-paying, hard-working member of a community who's just trying to survive the trials of everyday life. Citizens have a civic duty to say something when they see something unusual. You'll likely know it's unusual when you see it. Another civic duty of the law-abiding citizen is carrying a firearm on your person everywhere. Get some training and begin by protecting yourself and your family yourself, instead of delegating your responsibility elsewhere.

Many of us can become investigators in our own right too if we only apply ourselves. Furthermore, It might be a good idea to get one's eyes off our cell phones and start looking at what's happening around us and applying ourselves. I've never forgotten the wisdom in this quote:

"Evil exists because good people do nothing."

Don't be a sheep, but rather, be a sheepdog. Eyes forward, condition yellow always, attentive and aware. Watch out for your fellow men and women; in turn, they may be watching out for you. The Steven Koecher investigation is still ongoing. If I know James, I don't think he will give up pursuing more leads. Should you have something meaningful to contribute, or know something that could help move this case toward resolution, contact me at; *sighrep@yahoo.com*

In closing, I humbly pray Steven Koecher rests in peace and that his family has, to some degree, surmounted their grief over all this time.. And, may the St. George and Henderson police departments, and maybe even the FBI, take another hard look at this case. And may the person or persons responsible for his disappearance and death be held accountable, perchance with the assistance of a concerned citizen. Steven's car was not abandoned that day. It is Steven, and this case, which has been abandoned.

End

www.ingramcontent.com/pod-product-compliance
Lightning Source LLC
Chambersburg PA
CBHW070416120526
44590CB00014B/1412